Android™ Concurrency

About the Android Deep Dive Series

Zigurd Mednieks, Series Editor

The Android Deep Dive Series is for intermediate and expert developers who use Android Studio and Java, but do not have comprehensive knowledge of Android system-level programming or deep knowledge of Android APIs. Readers of this series want to bolster their knowledge of fundamentally important topics.

Each book in the series stands alone and provides expertise, idioms, frameworks, and engineering approaches. They provide in-depth information, correct patterns and idioms, and ways of avoiding bugs and other problems. The books also take advantage of new Android releases, and avoid deprecated parts of the APIs.

About the Series Editor

Zigurd Mednieks is a consultant to leading OEMs, enterprises, and entrepreneurial ventures creating Android-based systems and software. Previously he was chief architect at D2 Technologies, a voice-over-IP (VoIP) technology provider, and a founder of OpenMSobile, an Android-compatibility technology company. At D2 he led engineering and product definition work for products that blended communication and social media in purpose-built embedded systems and on the Android platform. He is lead author of *Programming Android* and *Enterprise Android*.

Android™ Concurrency

G. Blake Meike

✦ Addison-Wesley

Boston • Columbus • Indianapolis • New York • San Francisco • Amsterdam • Cape Town
Dubai • London • Madrid • Milan • Munich • Paris • Montreal • Toronto • Delhi
Mexico City • São Paulo • Sidney • Hong Kong • Seoul • Singapore • Taipei • Tokyo

Library of Congress Control Number: 2016937763

ISBN-13: 978-0-13-417743-4
ISBN-10: 0-13-417743-6

Text printed in the United States on recycled paper at RR Donnelley in Crawfordsville, Indiana
1   16

Editor-in-Chief
Greg Wiegand

Executive Editor
Laura Lewin

Development Editor
Sheri Replin

Managing Editor
Sandra Schroeder

Project Editor
Lori Lyons

Project Manager
Ellora Sengupta

Copy Editor
Abigail Manheim Bass

Indexer
Cheryl Lenser

Proofreader
Natarajan

Technical Reviewers
Joe Bowbeer
Thomas Kountis

Editorial Assistant
Olivia Basegio

Cover Designer
Chuti Prasertsith

Compositor
codeMantra

Graphics Conversion
Vived Graphics

❖

This book is for my mother, Sally Ann Obermeyer Meike, who encouraged me to be a snoot, long before David Foster Wallace re-purposed the term

❖

Contents at a Glance

NOTE: To register this product and gain access to bonus content, go to www.informit.com/register to sign in and enter the ISBN. After you register the product, a link to the additional content will be listed on your Account page, under Registered Products.

Table of Contents

Preface

I have had the opportunity during my years in working in this industry, to see concurrency in many contexts. When I was in school, it was a topic for dissertations. As a journeyman developer, I saw a lot of concurrent code, nearly all of it Java, in distributed back-end systems. Recently, I've had the opportunity to experience first-hand the turn to languages like Erlang and Scala, in the hope of making concurrent code easier to design and write.

I recall early in my career, being coached by a very supportive interviewer into reinventing double-checked locking. I certainly recall the furor, about a year later, when it was discovered that the double-checked locking idiom was not safe, and soon after, the first sighting of incorrect byte-code in the wild. Perhaps most surprising of all, though, I recently removed an implementation of the double-checked locking idiom from a piece of code written in 2015.

The constant, over this time, is the mystery and debate surrounding the topic. Perfectly competent novices suddenly balk or make naïve mistakes when concurrent code is necessary. Developers who are otherwise entirely reasonable sometimes disagree—occasionally quite vehemently—over the correctness of a particular piece of concurrent code. Their arguments, which may go on for hours, inevitably end up hinging on minutiae so fragile that the argument's actual winner is irrelevant.

I readily admit to feeling some kind of glee when I walked out of that early interview after having been led to double-checked locking. It was a shibboleth. I'd been initiated! Recently, I think I've seen the same kind of excitement in the faces of lecturers and their audiences as the lecturer passes on a secret: some fast and loose—and frequently downright incorrect—concurrency trick.

A really clever algorithm and a good shot of glee are wonderful things. We would all write better code, though, if we could strip some of the mystery and magic from concurrent programming. It would be great if instead of being the realm of the wizard, the correctness of a piece of concurrent code were something on which the opinions of two developers—even two developers with wildly different interests—rapidly converged.

Who Should Read This Book

This book is intended for developers with some experience with Android development.

If you are a novice developer, you will probably find some of the terms and concepts here unfamiliar. If you are a developer working on his or her very first Android app, you will probably be more concerned with simply getting familiar with the Android framework.

There are some really good books for you, already in existence, if you fit into either of these two categories. If that is the case, I encourage you to set this book aside for a while, enjoy the thrill of the steep part of a learning curve, and to come back when you have one complete Android app under your belt.

While it may sound obvious, I intend this book for reading. It is neither a cookbook nor a reference manual. I absolutely encourage you to try out the sample code. The examples are just sandboxes for experiments. Extend them. Try new experiments with them. Build your own personal understanding of the details of the Android OS. I hope, though, that you don't have to prop the book open next to your laptop to get value from it.

I was at one time bewitched by Perl. Looking back, I think that a major reason for that is that it was so much fun to read the Camel book (not the pink one, the blue one: the 2nd edition). I recall many enjoyable hours far from a keyboard and with no specific application in mind, simply reading that book.

I do not compare myself to Larry Wall. I do not by any means compare Android to Perl. I do hope, though, that you enjoy just reading this book. I hope that it is something that will make good company, perhaps on a plane flight or a long commute.

How This Book Is Organized

The first three chapters of this book will be a review for the audience for whom the book is intended.

I urge you not to skip Chapter 1, at least. It presents a model of concurrency that is somewhat atypical and that is the basis for the discussion in the following chapters.

Chapters 2 and 3 are intentionally short. They are a refresher for some basic ideas and provide an opportunity to reintroduce some common idioms. Experienced developers may choose to skim them.

Chapter 4 is a cautionary tale.

The heart of the book is Chapters 5 through 7. These chapters are a deep dive into some of the details of the Android operating system.

Chapter 8 is dessert: a bit of a how-to for some concurrency tools.

Example Code

Most of the code shown in examples in this book can be found on GitHub at https://github.com/AndroidConcurrencyDeepDive. If you experiment with them and discover something interesting or amusing, by all means submit a pull-request to share it with others.

Register your copy of *Android Concurrency* at informit.com for convenient access to downloads, updates, and corrections as they become available. To start the registration process, go to informit.com/register and log in or create an account. Enter the product ISBN 9780134177434 and click Submit. Once the process is complete, you will find any available bonus content under "Registered Products."

Conventions Used in This Book

The following typographical conventions are used in this book:

- **Bold** indicates new terms, URLs, email addresses, filenames, and file extensions.

- `Constant width` is used for program listings, as well as within paragraphs to refer to program elements such as variable or function names, databases, data types, environment variables, statements, and keywords.

- **`Constant width bold`** shows commands or other texts that should be typed by the user.

- `Constant width italic` shows texts that should be replaced with the user-supplied values or with the values determined by the context.

Note

A Note signifies a tip, suggestion, or general note.

About the Author

Blake Meike is a passionate engineer, architect, and code poet. As an author, speaker, and instructor, he has taught thousands of people how to write Android apps that aren't toys. He has more than 20 years of coding experience, most of it with Java, building systems as large as Amazon's massively scalable AutoScaling service and as small as a pre-Android OSS Linux/Java-based platform for cell phones. He is co-author of several other books, including O'Reilly's bestselling "Programming Android" and Wiley's "Enterprise Android." Blake holds a degree in Mathematics and Computer Science from Dartmouth College and was a founding member of Twitter University. He lives in Oakland, CA, and works for Cyanogen Inc.

Acknowledgements

This book owes its existence to a long list of contributors. My longtime colleague, Zigurd Mednieks, proposed it. Laura Lewin, Executive Editor at Pearson Technology Group, gave it a green light, and Carol Jelen, Literary Agent at Jelen Publishing, put a deal together.

The production staff at Pearson deftly turned the manuscript into a book. Illustrator Jenny Huckleberry cleaned up the figures and Development Editor Sheri Replin, Copy Editor Abigail Manheim Bass, and Project Editor Lori Lyons cleaned up the drafts. Editorial Assistant Olivia Basegio and Project Manager Ellora Sengupta kept us all together through the process. My thanks to all of you.

A special "thank you" and my eternal gratitude go to Laura Lewin, Executive Editor. Her patience with my complete inability to stick to any kind of schedule surely qualifies her for immediate sainthood.

On this book, my first as a solo author, my technical editors Joe Bowbeer, Thomas Kountis, and Zigurd Mednieks contributed so much that I am tempted to list them as co-authors. They were everything that I could have hoped for in a technical review team. Each, a recognized expert in the field, took the time to read carefully, understand, and then suggest changes as small as rewording and as big as re-thinking. While any remaining errors are strictly my own, any clarity and accuracy are due to them. I am incredibly lucky to have had their help. Thanks, guys!

Finally and always, thanks to my wonderful wife, Catherine, who endured yet another year of weekends with her husband on the couch, headphones on, incommunicado. That glitter heart is still for you, babe!

Understanding Concurrency

We propose to use the delays τ as absolute units of time which can be relied upon to synchronize the functions of various parts of the device.

John von Neumann

In order to build correct, concurrent Android programs, a developer needs a good model of concurrent processes, how they work, and what they are for. Concurrency actually isn't a big deal for most normal humans. For any multi-celled animal—arguably even for viruses—it is just normal existence. It is only those of us obsessed with computers that give a second thought to the idea of walking and chewing gum at the same time.

Concurrency Made Hard

Walking and chewing gum isn't easy in the strange world of Dr. John von Neumann. In his 1945 paper, "The First Draft Report on the EDVAC" (von Neumann 1954), he describes the architecture of one of the very first electronic digital computers. In most ways, that architecture has changed very little in the seventy years since. Throughout their history, digital computers have been, roughly speaking, gigantic balls of state that are transformed, over time, by a sequence of well-defined operations. Time and order are intrinsic parts of the definition of the machine.

Most of computer science has been the discussion of clever sequences of operations that will transform one machine state into another, more desirable, state. As modern machines commonly have more than 10^{14} possible states, those discussions are already barely manageable. If the order in which transformations take place can vary, the discussion necessarily broadens to include all possible combinations of all possible states, and becomes utterly impossible. Sequential execution is the law of the land.

Concurrency in Software

Of course, computer languages are written for humans. They are intended to help us express an algorithm (the sequence of instructions that transforms the machine state) efficiently, correctly, and, perhaps, even in a way that future human readers can understand.

Early programming languages were, essentially, an extension of the hardware. Even today many are reflections of the machine architecture they were originally designed to control. Nearly all of them are **procedural** and consist of lists of instructions for changing (**mutating**) the state of memory. Because it is simply too difficult to reason about all of the possible states of that memory, languages have, over time, become more and more restrictive about the state changes they allow a developer to express. One way to look at the history of programming language design is as a quest for a system that allows developers to express correct algorithms easily, and not express incorrect ones at all.

The very first languages were machine languages—code that translated, one-for-one, into instructions for the computer. These languages were undesirable for two reasons. First, expressing even a very simple idea might take tens of lines of code. Second, it was much too easy to express errors.

Over time, in order to restrict and manage the ways in which a program could change state, languages have narrowed the choices. Most, for instance, restrict program execution from arbitrarily skipping around between instructions to using now-familiar conditionals, loops, and procedure calls. Modules and eventually OOP (Object-Oriented Programming) followed, as ways of separating a program into small, understandable pieces and then limiting the way those pieces can interact. This modularized, building-block approach makes modern languages more abstract and expressive. Some even have well-developed type systems that help prevent errors. Almost all of them, though, are still imperative: lists of instructions for changing machine state.

Functional Programming

While most computer research and development focused on doing more and more complicated things, on bigger and faster hardware based on von Neumann architecture, a small but persistent contingent has pursued a completely different idea: *functional programming*.

A purely functional program differs from a procedural program in that it does not have mutable state. Instead of reasoning about successive changes to machine state, functional languages reason about evaluating functions at given parameters. This is a fairly radical idea and it takes some thinking to understand how it could work. If it were possible, though, it would have some very appealing aspects from a concurrency point of view. In particular, if there is no mutable state, there is no implicit time or order. If there is no implicit order, then concurrency is just an uninteresting tautology.

John McCarthy introduced Lisp, the first functional language, in 1958, only a year or two after the creation of the first commonly accepted procedural language, Fortran. Since then, Lisp and its functional relatives (Scheme, ML, Haskel, Erlang, and so on) have been variously dismissed as brilliant but impractical, as educational tools, or as shibboleths for hipster developers. Now that Moore's law (Moore, 1965) is more likely to predict the number of processors on a chip than the speed of a single processor, people are not dismissing functional languages anymore. (By 1975, Moore formalized this concept when he revised his original thoughts, and said the number of integrated circuit (IC) components would double every two years.)

Programming in a functional style is an important strategy for concurrent programming and may become more important in the future. Java, the language of Android, does not qualify as a functional language and certainly does not support the complex type system associated with most functional languages.

Language as Contract

Functional or procedural, a programming language is an abstraction. Only a tiny fraction of developers need to get anywhere near machine language these days. Even that tiny fraction is probably writing code in a virtual instruction set, implemented by a software virtual machine, or by chip firmware. The only developers likely to understand the precise behavior of the instruction set for a particular piece of hardware, in detail, are the ones writing compilers for it.

It follows that a developer, writing a program in some particular language, expects to understand the behavior of that program by making assertions in that language. A developer reasons in the language in which the program is written—the abstraction—and almost never needs to demonstrate that a program is correct (or incorrect) by examining the actual machine code. She might reason, for instance, that something happens 14 times because the loop counter is initialized to 13, decremented each time through the loop, and the loop is terminated when the counter reaches 0.

This is important because most of our languages are imperative (not functional) abstractions. Even though hardware, registers, caches, instructions pipelines, and clock cycles typically don't come up during program design, when we reason about our programs we are, nonetheless, reasoning about sequence.

Concurrency in Hardware

It is supremely ironic that procedural languages, originally reflections of the architecture they were designed to control, no longer represent the behavior of computer hardware. Although the CPU of an early computer might have been capable of only a single operation per tick of its internal clock, all modern processors are performing multiple tasks simultaneously. It would make no sense at all to idle even a quarter of the transistors on a 4-billion gate IC while waiting for some single operation to complete.

Why Is Everything Sequential?

It is possible that sequential execution is just an inherent part of how we humans understand things. Perhaps we first imposed it on our hardware design and then perpetuated it in our language design because it is a reflection of the way our minds work.

Hardware is physical stuff. It is part of the real world, and the real world is most definitely not sequential. Modern hardware is very parallel.

In addition to running on parallel processors, modern programs are more and more frequently interacting with a wildly parallel world. The owners of even fairly ordinary feature-phones are constantly multitasking: listening to music while browsing the web, or answering the phone call that suddenly arrives. They expect the phone to keep up. At the same time, sensors, hardware buttons, touch screens, and microphones are all simultaneously sending data to programs. Maintaining the illusion of "sequentiality" is quite a feat.

A developer is in an odd position. As shown in Figure 1.1, she is building a set of instructions for a sequential abstraction that will run on a highly parallel processor for a program that will interact with a parallel world.

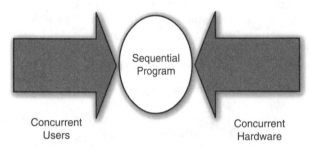

Figure 1.1   A sequential program in a concurrent world

Concurrency Made Simple

The purpose of the discussion, up to this point, has been to reframe the idea of concurrency. Concurrency is not a way to make a program run faster. It is not a complex juggling trick that ninja coders use to keep multiple balls in the air at one time. On the contrary, it is the apparent sequential execution of a program that is the complex trick. Sequential execution is an illusion maintained by a cabal of compiler writers and hardware architects. Concurrency is simply the relaxation of a fabricated constraint.

Threads

In the developer's environment, where time and order are rigid and implicit constraints, "concurrency" is just another word for "order unspecified"—the way things are everywhere else. A concurrent program is just one that announces to an already-concurrent world that its correctness does not depend on the ordering of events that occur in separate components. In a concurrent program, those separate, partially ordered components are called **threads of execution**, or just **threads**. Within a thread, instructions are still executed in rigidly sequential order. The order of execution of instructions in two separate threads, however, is completely unspecified.

In the early days of computing, the choice of threads as a model for concurrency was not obvious. Developers that needed out-of-order processing were forced to brew their own concurrency constructs. Both literature and code from the 1960s contain a wide variety of models for asynchronous execution.

Threads probably originated in the late 1960s, with IBM's OS/360. They were called "tasks," and were an OS-level service that saved developers the trouble of building their own concurrency abstraction. In 1991 Java, called Oak at the time, adopted the thread model and supported it in the language, even on operating systems that did not.

Even today, threads are not the only model for concurrency. Languages such as Erlang, Go, and Clojure, for instance, each use an entirely different model.

Introducing threads into the programming model does not present an intrinsic problem. Operating two cars in parallel causes no problems unless they both try to occupy the same space at the same time. Similarly, operating two threads that are completely independent is also perfectly safe. There are millions of programs, each concurrently running in its own thread of execution on millions of separate computers, at this very moment. Most of these programs don't interact with each other in any way and their behavior is perfectly well defined. The problems only arise when threads need to share state and resources.

Atomic Execution

When multiple threads change state that is accessible to both, the results can easily be nondeterministic. Because there is no relationship between the order in which statements are executed, subtle changes in timing can change the result of running the program.

Consider the following code:

```
executionCount++;
someTask();
```

Just by inspection, it seems likely that the variable executionCount is meant to count the number of times that the function someTask is called. In a concurrent environment, however, this code, as it stands, does not have deterministic behavior because the ++ operation is not atomic—it is not a single, indivisible action. Table 1.1 demonstrates an execution sequence that fails to record one execution.

Table 1.1 **Non-Atomic Execution**

executionCount = 4

Thread 1	Thread 2
read execution count (4)	read execution count (4)
increment (5)	increment (5)
store execution count (5)	store execution count (5)
call someTask	call someTask

Synchronization is the basic mechanism through which multiple Java threads share state in such a way that the result of the interaction is deterministic. In itself, synchronization is a simple idea: a **critical section** of code is protected by a mutual-exclusion lock or **mutex**. When a thread enters the critical section—that is, it begins executing instructions from it—it is said to seize the mutex. No other thread can enter the section until the first thread leaves.

The previous code becomes deterministic if only a single thread is allowed to execute the critical section at any given time:

```
synchronized(this) {
    executionCount++;
    someTask();
}
```

Synchronization is the crux of creating correct concurrent Java programs, and is the basis for a lot of things that are definitely not simple. Those things make up the content of the rest of this book.

Visibility

There is one more thing, however, that is simple. Remember that the previous example is an abstraction! It is written in a computer language—Java, in this case—and is, therefore, related to the actual behavior of hardware only by the grace of compiler writers, JVM developers, and hardware architects. Those two Java statements translate into hundreds of microinstructions, many of them executed in parallel, over tens of hardware clock cycles. The illusion that there are two statements, happening in order, is no more than an illusion.

Maintaining the illusion is not something that near-the-metal developers do naturally. On the contrary, they find sequential programs naive, clumsy, and wasteful. They are only too happy to fix them by re-ordering instructions, executing multiple instructions in parallel, representing a single piece of program state as multiple copies, and so on. By doing so, they do their very best to make optimal use of the immense power of the multiple processors that comprise even the tiny devices we carry in our pockets.

In general, we're glad to have them perform these optimizations. They make our programs run faster, on multiple hardware platforms, using tricks in which application developers are just not that interested. There is one important condition on this optimization, however: *They must not break the illusion of sequentiality!* In other words, compilers and hardware pipelines can reorder and parallelize all they want to optimize the code, as long as developers can't tell that they did it.

In making a program concurrent, a developer clearly states that there is no sequential dependency between the states controlled by different threads. If there is no sequential dependency, a compiler should be free to perform all sorts of optimizations that would otherwise have been unsafe. Without an explicit ordering between events in different threads, the compiler is free to make changes in the execution sequence of one thread without any consideration of the statements in any other.

A correct concurrent program is one that abides by the contract for maintaining an illusion. Negotiation between application programmers and hardware developers produce a language, and that language is a contract. The application developers get their illusion of sequential execution, something about which they can reason. The hardware developers get a toolbox of clever tricks they can use to make programs run fast. In the middle is the contract.

In Java, that contract is called the **memory model**. On one side of the contract is the application programmer, reasoning about her program in a high-level language. On the other side of the contract are the compiler writers, virtual machine developers, and hardware architects, moving everything that isn't explicitly forbidden. Developers who talk about hardware when discussing concurrency are missing the point. A correct concurrent program is not about hardware; it is about developers keeping their end of the contract.

Fortunately, in Java, the contract is easily stated. The following single sentence states it almost completely:

> Whenever more than one thread accesses a given state variable, and one of them might write to it, they all must coordinate their access to it using synchronization.
>
> (Göetz, et al. 2006)

A correct concurrent Java program is one that abides by this contract—no more, no less. Note in particular that whether a thread reads or writes mutable state does not affect its need for synchronization in any way.

Summary

Concurrency itself is nothing to be scared of. We all deal with it in the real world, all day, every day. What is difficult is writing concurrent programs for computers based on mutable state. It is difficult because the concept of order is such an important implicit basis for the way we reason about our programs.

Concurrency is the relaxation of the rigid order inherent in imperative computer languages. Java's mechanism for doing this is the thread. A thread executes instructions in an order that is not related to the order of execution of instructions in other threads. Developers use mutual exclusion locks (mutexes) to control thread access to critical sections of code, thereby limiting the number of ways that two different threads can execute instructions in the section.

Most of today's computer languages manufacture an illusion of sequential execution. Behind the scenes, however, they fiercely reorder, parallelize, and cache to make the best use of hardware. The only thing that prevents those optimizations from making a program behave non-deterministically, is a contract. A correct program is one that abides by that contract.

No one ever said that concurrency was easy. It is, however, fairly simple. Just follow the contract.

2

Java Concurrency

Whenever more than one thread accesses a given state variable, and one of them might write to it, they all must coordinate their access to it using synchronization.

Brian Göetz

Java is one of the earliest languages in which concurrency is native. Built into the language at a low level are the constructs necessary for creating concurrent programs. In addition, as Java was conceived to be portable across multiple hardware architectures, it was also one of the first to define a memory model and to specify the exact behavior of its concurrent constructs.

Because Android's concurrency constructs are built on Java's, this chapter is a review of basic Java concurrency mechanisms. Of course, a complete description of the concurrency in Java can and does fill many complete books. The intention here is simply to establish vocabulary and refresh memory.

> **Note**
>
> Probably the best resource for concurrent programming in Java is the book from which this chapter's introductory quote is taken: Java Concurrency in Practice, Göetz and Peierls, et al. Anyone who plans to do any substantial amount of concurrent programming in Java—and this includes all Android developers—should read this book.

Java Threads

In Java, the class `Thread` implements a thread. Every running application has one implicit thread, usually called the "default" or "main" thread. Spawning a new thread consists of creating a new instance of the `Thread` class and then calling its `start` method.

> **Note**
>
> In Android, the "main" thread is also frequently called the "UI" thread because it powers most of the UI components. This name can be confusing. There are actually multiple threads that run the UI and the main thread powers even applications that have no UI components.

The Thread Class

The two `Thread` methods `start` and `run` are very special. The `start` method takes no parameters and returns no values. From the point of view of the calling code, it doesn't do anything at all. It just returns and passes control to the next statement in the program.

The magic, though, is that the call actually returns twice, once to the next statement in the program, but also on a new thread of execution spawned by the call, in the `Thread` object's `run` method. The new thread executes the statements in the `run` method, in order, until the method returns. When the `run` method returns, the new thread is terminated.

Listing 2.1 is a simple example of the use of a Java Thread.

Listing 2.1 **Spawning a Thread**

```
public class ThreadedExample {
    public static void main(String... args) {
        System.out.println("starting: " + Thread.currentThread());
        new Thread() {
            @Override
            public void run() {
                System.out.println("running: " + Thread.currentThread());
            }
        }.start();
        System.out.println("finishing: " + Thread.currentThread());
    }
}
```

This program, when run, will print the three messages and then terminate. It defines an anonymous subclass of `Thread` that overrides its run method. The overridden method is executed on a new thread, out of order with the execution of the thread that called the `start` method.

An example of the output from one run of the programs demonstrates this:

```
starting: Thread[main,5,main]
finishing: Thread[main,5,main]
running: Thread[Thread-0,5,main]
```

Notice that the message printed from within the `run` method verifies that the current thread within the new thread's `run` method is not the thread that executes the other two print statements.

In what order will the three messages appear? The "starting" message will always appear first. Java guarantees a happened-before edge between any statement that precedes the call to the `start` method for a new thread in program order, and any statement in the new thread. In other words, everything happens in program order until the new thread starts and the new thread sees the world as it was at the time it was started.

There is no guarantee about the ordering of the remaining two messages. They will both be printed but Java does not define which will appear first. For some particular implementations of Java running on some specific hardware, the two messages might even appear in one order or the other most of the time. It would be quite incorrect, though, to take the fact that the messages happen to appear in a particular order each time the program is actually run, as evidence that they will always appear in that order. The two messages are unordered with respect to one another.

Furthermore, were the print methods not thread-safe, it would even be possible that the two messages could be interspersed: that the output produced by the running program would be an unreadable combination of the two messages.

Runnables

Although the previous example, a sub-classed Thread, is the simplest way to create a new thread of execution, it is not necessarily the best. Given Java's constraint for single implementation inheritance, it would be a great shame to require that anything that needs to run on a new thread must also be a subclass of Thread. Indeed, that is not a requirement.

When an implementation of the Runnable interface is passed to a new Thread object, on creation, the Thread's default run method calls that Runnable's run method. Listing 2.2 shows a different implementation that behaves exactly like the previous example. Although it might not be immediately apparent in Listing 2.2, this example is quite a bit more flexible because the Runnable could inherit behavior from an arbitrary super-class.

Listing 2.2 **Thread with Runnable**

```java
public class RunnableExample {
    public static void main(String... args) {
        System.out.println("starting: " + Thread.currentThread());
        new Thread(new Runnable() {
            @Override
            public void run() {
                System.out.println("running: " + Thread.currentThread());
            }
        }).start();
        System.out.println("finishing: " + Thread.currentThread());
    }
}
```

Synchronization

As mentioned in the previous chapter, synchronization is the mechanism through which a group of statements is made atomic: only a single thread can execute statements in the block controlled by the synchronization lock—the critical section—at any given time. In Java synchronization is accomplished using the synchronized keyword and an object used as a mutex. The language guarantees that, at most, one thread can execute the statements in a given synchronized block at any time.

> **Note**
>
> The three words mutex, monitor, and lock are used nearly interchangeably here. **Mutex** is perhaps the most clearly defined. It is a lock that provides mutual exclusion: only one thread may hold it at a time. The Java Specification uses the word **monitor** to describe an instance whose associated mutex is used to control access to a synchronized block. **Lock** is a looser term, with a more intuitive meaning.

Mutexes

Although threads are special objects, in Java any object can be used as a mutex for a synchronized block. Every Java `Object` has a monitor.

Listing 2.3 demonstrates a simple use of the synchronized keyword.

Listing 2.3 **Synchronizing on an Object**

```
public class SynchronizedExample {
    static final Object lock = new Object();

    public static void main(String... args) {
        System.out.println("starting: " + Thread.currentThread());
        new Thread(new Runnable() {
            @Override
            public void run() {
                synchronized (lock) {
                    System.out.println("running: " + Thread.currentThread());
                }
            }
        }).start();

        synchronized (lock) {
            System.out.println("finishing: " + Thread.currentThread());
        }
    }
}
```

The critical sections in Listing 2.3 are the two print statements inside the two synchronized blocks. The object used as a monitor, `lock`, is nothing special. It is just an instance of the simplest of all objects, `Object`, created early in the code.

It can take some analysis to understand how the use of synchronization affects the example. There is, after all, only one thread that ever has the opportunity to execute the `run` method of the anonymous `Runnable`: the thread created in the anonymous thread's `start` method. Similarly, there is only one thread that can print the "finishing" message: the main thread. If only one thread can enter either critical section, perhaps the synchronization is pointless?

In the unsynchronized version of this program, the new thread might print the "running" message at exactly the same time that the main thread prints the "finishing" message. If the print methods were not synchronized internally, this might result in an unreadable garble of the two messages. Because both synchronized blocks in the code in Listing 2.3 use the same mutex object, however, this version of the program cannot intermingle the two messages. Even though there are two separate synchronized blocks, only one thread can hold the mutex on a given object at any time.

One of the two threads, T1, will seize the mutex for the monitor object, enter one of the critical sections and print a message. Because it is holding the mutex, the other thread, T2, will not be able to enter its critical section. T2 will wait on the lock, at the beginning of its critical section, until T1 releases it. When T1 releases the lock, T2 will be notified that it can proceed. It will then enter its critical section, print its message, and continue.

Notice that that this synchronized version of the application still does not define the order in which the two messages will appear. There is no way to tell which of the two program threads, the main thread or the new thread, will enter its critical section first. This example, like the one before it, is said to contain a **race condition**.

Synchronizing on `this`

Because every object has a monitor, a convenient object on which to synchronize within a method is `this`. It makes sense that an object that must synchronize access to its state would do so by synchronizing on itself.

Listing 2.4 is an example of this technique. The `Runnable` is still an instance of an anonymous class. In this version of the program, however, a reference to the instance is stored in the variable `job`. The synchronization on `this`, from within the anonymous runnable's `run` method, and the synchronization on `job`, in the main method, are synchronizing on the same object. This version behaves identically to the version in Listing 2.3.

Listing 2.4 **Synchronizing on** This

```
public class SynchronizedThisExample {
    private static final Runnable job = new Runnable() {
        @Override
        public void run() {
            synchronized (this) {
                System.out.println("running: " + Thread.currentThread());
            }
        }
    };

    public static void main(String... args) {
        System.out.println("starting: " + Thread.currentThread());
        new Thread(job).start();
        synchronized (job) {
            System.out.println("finishing: " + Thread.currentThread());
        }
    }
}
```

> **Note**
>
> Experts will note that, though accurate, Listing 2.4 is not an improvement on Listing 2.3. Synchronizing the entire method, as in Listing 2.5, is a step backward in granularity that undermines most of the purpose of multithreading.

Synchronized Methods

Java has shorthand for synchronizing on `this`. Using the `synchronized` keyword in the signature of a method is exactly the same as wrapping the method's contents in a block synchronized on `this`. For instance, the two methods `sync1` and `sync2` shown in Listing 2.5 are identical.

Listing 2.5 **Synchronized Methods**

```java
public class SynchronizedMethodExample {
    private int executionCount;

    public synchronized void sync1() {
        executionCount++;
        someTask();
    }

    public void sync2() {
        synchronized (this) {
            executionCount++;
            someTask();
        }
    }

    private void someTask() {
        // ...
    }
}
```

A static method qualified with a `synchronized` keyword is synchronized on its class object. The two methods in Listing 2.6 are also identical to one another.

Listing 2.6 **Synchronized Static Methods**

```java
public class SynchronizedStaticExample {
    private static int executionCount;

    public static synchronized void sync1() {
        executionCount++;
        someTask();
    }
```

```
public static void sync2() {
    synchronized (SynchronizedStaticExample.class) {
        executionCount++;
        someTask();
    }
}

private static void someTask() {
    // ...
}
}
```

Reentrant Monitors

Object monitors are said to be **reentrant**. Although only one thread can hold a mutex at any given time, once the thread holds it, successive attempts by the same thread to seize it again are, essentially, no-ops. Listing 2.7 shows a program that synchronizes twice on the same monitor, this. The program will complete successfully. It is correct, if not useful.

Listing 2.7   **Synchronized Static Methods**

```
public class ReentrantLockingExample {

    public static void main(String... args) {
        new ReentrantLockingExample().run1();
    }

    private synchronized void run1() { run2(); }

    private synchronized void run2() {
        System.out.println("reentrant locks!");
    }
}
```

Common Synchronization Errors

Incorrect synchronization is the most common error in concurrent programs. Unfortunately, there's a lot more to it than just getting the right things into synchronized blocks.

Using a Single Mutex

Access to a critical section is atomic only if the section synchronizes on a single mutex. It is the mutex, not the block, that protects the code.

Although locking on `this` is convenient, experienced developers may recognize that synchronization on a single object, `this`, might serialize operations that could otherwise be concurrent. An object, for instance, that has state components that are updated by requests to independent network endpoints might be significantly optimized if the requests do not block each other. To keep the separate operations from interfering with each other, the object might use separate locks to control access to separate components. Unfortunately, that might lead to code like that shown in Listing 2.8. See if you can identify the problem.

Listing 2.8 **The Wrong Mutex**

```
public class LeakingLockExample {
    private String title = "";

    public void setTitle(String title) {
        if (null == title) {
            throw new NullPointerException("title may not be null");
        }
        synchronized (this.title) { this.title = title; }
    }
}
```

Of course, the problem is that the assignment to `this.title` is not correctly synchronized.

In the example, two different threads can see the assignment to `this.title` protected by different mutexes. Thread T1 seizes the mutex on the string currently referenced by `this.title`. As soon as it assigns `this.title` though, thread T2 can enter the `setTitle` method, and seize a different mutex. Because the two threads have not synchronized on a single mutex, there is no happens-before edge between them and the code could behave in any of a number of ways.

Deadlock

The second most common category of errors in concurrent programs is the deadlock. The previous discussion of Reentrant Monitors pointed out that attempting to seize the same mutex twice does not hang the thread. With two or more mutexes, though, it is quite possible to create code through which, under the right circumstances, no thread can make forward progress.

A deadlock occurs when two or more threads each holds locks that the other needs. This can happen, for instance, if threads T1 and T2 both need access to resources R1 and R2, which are protected by locks L1 and L2, respectively. If T1 seizes L1 to get access to R1 at the same time that T2 seizes L2 to get access to R2, neither T1 nor T2 will ever make forward progress. T1 needs L2, but cannot get it because it is held by T2. T2 needs L1 but cannot get it because it is held by T1. Listing 2.9 is an example of a program that might deadlock.

Listing 2.9   **Deadlock**

```
public class DeadlockingExample {
    static final Object lock1 = new Object();
    static final Object lock2 = new Object();

    public static void main(String... args) {
        System.out.println("starting: " + Thread.currentThread());

        new Thread(new Runnable() {
            @Override
            public void run() {
                synchronized (lock1) {
                    synchronized (lock2) {
                        System.out.println("running: " + Thread.currentThread());
                    }
                }
            }
        }).start();

        synchronized (lock2) {
            synchronized (lock1) {
                System.out.println("finishing: " + Thread.currentThread());
            }
        }
    }
}
```

Volatile

Most developers understand the need for atomicity in a concurrent program—and how to use synchronization to assure it—fairly easily. As discussed in Chapter 1, a much more common misunderstanding has to do with visibility. That misunderstanding frequently manifests itself in the belief that it is necessary to synchronize writing mutable state but not reading it. Listing 2.10 is an example of this kind of error.

Listing 2.10   **Incorrect Synchronization**

```
public class IncorrectSynchronizationExample {
    static boolean stop;

    private static final Runnable job = new Runnable() {
        @Override
        public void run() {
            while (!stop) {   // !!! Incorrect!
```

```
                System.out.println("running: " + Thread.currentThread());
            }
        }
    };

    public static void main(String... args) {
        System.out.println("starting: " + Thread.currentThread());

        new Thread(job).start();

        synchronized (job) {  // !!! Incorrect!
            System.out.println("finishing: " + Thread.currentThread());
            stop = true;
        }
    }
}
```

This code is incorrect. The use of synchronization for only one thread accomplishes nothing.

The reasoning behind this kind of code is usually something along the lines of: "There's nothing critical about the number of times the loop in the run method is executed. If it runs 2 or 7 extra times, before it notices the stop flag, nobody cares... and without synchronization, it will run much more efficiently."

Remember, though, in the short description of Java's contract that heads this chapter, that it is just the *potential* for write access from any thread that affects the need for synchronization There is no happened-before relationship of any kind between the assignment to stop on the main thread and the read from it, on the spawned thread. A cause in one need not ever result in an effect in the other.

As an example of a way in which this program might fail, consider a compiled version of the code in which the variable stop was represented as a register. Now suppose that the two threads are run on two separate cores in a CPU. There might well be two completely different stop flags, each a register in a different core. A change in the value of one is visible in the other only if the generated code forces the synchronization of the two values. That synchronization is expensive, and without the indication that it is necessary, might be optimized away. The spawned thread can run until it is externally terminated.

To reiterate, correct concurrency is about a contract. Although this example discusses hardware and compilers to demonstrate an error, attempting to demonstrate the absence of an error by citing known hardware and compiler architecture is fallacious reasoning. The memory model is the law. Programs that do not abide by it are incorrect.

The visibility problem in Listing 2.10 can be fixed with the addition of a single keyword, volatile. A variable marked as volatile behaves as if every reference to it were wrapped in a synchronization block. Listing 2.11 shows the corrected program.

Listing 2.11   **Volatile**

```
public class VolatileExample {
    static volatile boolean stop;

    private static final Runnable job = new Runnable() {
        @Override
        public void run() {
            while (!stop) {
                System.out.println("running: " + Thread.currentThread());
            }
        }
    };

    public static void main(String... args) {
        System.out.println("starting: " + Thread.currentThread());

        new Thread(job).start();

        System.out.println("finishing: " + Thread.currentThread());
        stop = true;
    }
}
```

This program, like the ones in Listings 2.2 and 2.3, could possibly garble the messages if message printing were not synchronized. If the main thread changes the state of the stop flag, though, the spawned thread is guaranteed to see the change.

Note that making the stop flag volatile does not guarantee that the program will terminate! There is nothing, even in this version, that guarantees that the stop flag will ever be set to true. Because there is no ordering specified between the two threads, one entirely legal scenario is that the second thread is started and the first suspended and never resumed. In this scenario, the second thread is said to **starve** the first.

When there are not enough processors to power all the threads in a program, some kind of scheduler must assign those processors to threads. Hopefully it does that in a way that gives each thread a "fair share." In practice, with the scheduler for the Android platform, Java's lax scheduling rules are very rarely a concern. Even on Android, though, the exact meaning of "fair share" can, occasionally, be surprising.

Also note that although it does provide visibility, the volatile keyword does not provide atomicity. The program in Listing 2.12 might not print exactly eleven messages. As described in the previous chapter, the ++ operator is not atomic and it is possible for the read-alter-rewrite to store an incorrect value.

Listing 2.12   **Incorrect Volatile**

```java
public class VolatileExample {
    static volatile int iterations;

    private static final Runnable job = new Runnable() {
        @Override
        public void run() {
            while (iterations++ < 10) {
                System.out.println("running: " + Thread.currentThread());
            }
        }
    };

    public static void main(String... args) {
        System.out.println("starting: " + Thread.currentThread());

        new Thread(job).start();

        while (iterations++ < 10) {
            System.out.println("finishing: " + Thread.currentThread());
        }
    }
}
```

Wait and Notify

Java contains two other concurrency primitives, the methods `wait` and `notifyAll`. The `notifyAll` method also has a less-frequently-used variant, `notify`.

Wait

The `wait` method enables a thread that has entered a synchronized block by seizing its mutex, to pause and release the mutex while still within block. This does not violate atomicity because, although the thread is inside the synchronized block, it is suspended and not executing.

The `wait` method can be called only when the current thread holds the mutex for the object on which the `wait` method is called. Listing 2.13 will throw a `java.lang.IllegalMonitorStateException` because the `wait` method is called when the executing thread does not hold the monitor object, `lock`.

Listing 2.13   **IllegalMonitorStateException**

```
public class WaitExceptionExample {
    private Object lock = new Object();
    public static void main(String... args) {
        try { lock.wait(); }
        catch (InterruptedException e) {
            throw new AssertionError("Interrupts not supported");
        }
    }
}
```

When a thread is executing inside a synchronized block, and it calls the `wait` method on the block's monitor object, the thread is suspended and releases the monitor. A thread that is suspended in a call to `wait` can be rescheduled by a subsequent call to `notify` or `notifyAll`. Of course, that call will have to be made from another thread; the suspended thread cannot do anything until it is rescheduled.

The code shown in Listing 2.14 contains two synchronized blocks that together control the number of threads executing the call to `req.run`.

When a new thread—this time let's call it Edsger—enters the first critical section, the code checks to see whether there are already too many requests running. If there are not, Edsger increments the running count, leaves the critical section, and runs its request. When it completes the request, it attempts to enter the second critical section.

If any other thread is executing either of the two critical sections, Edsger will have to wait for that other thread either to leave, or to call `wait`. Once that happens Edsger enters the second critical section, decrements the count of running requests, and exits the method.

Consider, though, what would happen if three other threads (perhaps named Tony, Niklaus, and Per Brinch) were already running requests when Edsger entered the first synchronized block. Because the running count is already at its maximum, Edsger enters a loop that it can leave only when the running count goes below the maximum. Note that at this point Edsger is not yet counted as running. The running count can go below the maximum in only one way: some other thread that is currently running a request must enter the second synchronized block and decrement the count. Because Edsger releases the monitor when it calls `wait`, other threads are able do this.

> **Note**
>
> Among the things that are out of scope for this chapter is a complete discussion of the complex subject of handling of thread interrupts. In the examples here, interruptions are specifically disallowed. Brian Göetz has a good article on how to handle them correctly here: http://www.ibm.com/developerworks/library/j-jtp05236/.

Notify

Another thread decrementing the running count, however, won't restart Edsger. Once a thread waits for a particular monitor, it will not be scheduled again, even if it could run, unless some running thread calls either `notifyAll` or `notify` for the same monitor. Listing 2.14 does this in the second critical section.

It is only when the running count is at its maximum that it is possible that threads are waiting in the first critical section; therefore `notifyAll`, in the second critical section, is called only then.

The distinction between the two methods, `notify` and `notifyAll`, is very important. A call to `notify` reschedules exactly one thread that is waiting on the monitor; `notifyAll` reschedules all of them. This is significant when different threads are waiting for different reasons.

Listing 2.14 **Using Wait and Notify**

```
public static final int RUN_MAX = 3;
private final Object lock = new Object();
private int running;

public void rateLimiter(NetworkRequest req) {
  synchronized (lock) {
    while (running >= RUN_MAX) {
      try { lock.wait(); }
      catch (InterruptedException e) {
        throw new AssertionError("Interrupts not supported");
      }
    }
    running++;
  }
  try { req.run(); }
  finally {
    synchronized (lock) {
      if (running-- == RUN_MAX) { lock.notify(); }
    }
  }
}
```

Consider what would happen if the code in Listing 2.14 were modified to enable two different running maximums, one for threads that were performing read requests and another for those doing write requests. Suppose that the running count for readers went below its maximum, forcing a call to `notify`. It is entirely possible that only a thread waiting to write would be rescheduled, only to discover that although the read running count was below its maximum, the running count for writing was still above its maximum. The write thread might wait once again without ever notifying any other thread. In this case, no reading thread—no thread that can make forward progress—is ever rescheduled.

In circumstances like this, when different threads are waiting for different things, it is essential to call notifyAll, not notify. The former, as its name implies, reschedules all the threads waiting for the monitor. This is somewhat more expensive: each thread wakes up, examines the environment, and either proceeds or calls wait again if it cannot get the resources it needs. Only when threads are indistinguishable, as they are in Listing 2.14, is it safe to use notify. Even then, though, it is advisable to use notifyAll as a means of future-proofing.

The Concurrency Package

Although it is useful to understand Java's low-level concurrency constructs, most code should never use any of them. Most code is concerned with accomplishing much higher-level goals. For most applications, designing with wait and notify is like planning a trip from San Francisco to Boston by considering carburetor design.

In Java 5, Java introduced an addition to the java.util package containing a framework of higher-level concurrency abstractions. Like the Collections framework before it, the Concurrency framework is safe, powerful, and sufficient for most programming tasks. Code that contains calls to low-level constructs like wait and notify is probably doing it wrong.

Safe Publication

A key problem in concurrent programming is sharing data between threads. Transferring data correctly from one thread to another is called **safe publication**. A careful examination of the rule that heads this chapter reveals a couple of strategies for safe publication.

The simplest strategy is immutable data. If it is impossible for any thread to change the state of the data, then the antecedent of the concurrency rule does not apply, and sharing the data is safe. As a rule of thumb, in Java, for state to be immutable it should be declared final. "Java Concurrency in Practice" (Göetz, et al. 2006) introduced the concept of "effective immutability" to discuss the situation in which everyone agrees not to change a variable's value. That certainly works. It is much safer, however, to use the language to guarantee that a variable's value cannot be changed, than to rely on assurances that it won't be.

Transferring mutable state between threads is ticklish business. Fortunately, there is a standard idiom for doing it. Figure 2.1 illustrates that idiom.

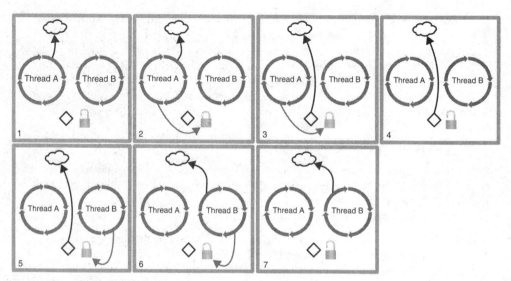

Figure 2.1   A safe publication idiom

When Thread A wants to pass an object to Thread B, it makes use of a mutex and a drop box. Thread A seizes the mutex and then puts a reference to the object into the drop box. It must make certain that it no longer holds any references to the transferred object. Thread A then releases the mutex. Thread B seizes the mutex and recovers the object reference from the drop box. Thread B must make certain that the drop box no longer holds a reference to the object before it releases the mutex.

Listing 2.15 is a partial implementation of the safe publication algorithm, in Java.

Listing 2.15   **Safe Publication**

```java
private Object lock = new Object();
private T dropBox;

/**
 * Safely publish an object to another thread.
 *
 * @param obj The caller must hold <b>no other references</b> to this object.
 */
public void publish(T obj) {
  synchronized (lock) {
    if (null != dropBox) {
      throw new IllegalStateException("The drop box is full!");
    }
    dropBox = obj;
  }
}
```

```
/**
 * Receive a published object.
 *
 * @return the received object
 */
public T receive() {
  synchronized (lock) {
    T obj = dropBox;
    dropBox = null;
    return obj;
  }
}
```

During this transfer, there is only one piece of mutable state that is shared by two threads: the drop box. The object being passed is at no time accessible from more than one thread. A single mutex controls access to the drop box and the transfer is, therefore, safe and correct.

In common use, this idiom is implemented using a queue, instead of a simple drop box. Threads exchange data by enqueuing an object and leaving it to be dequeued by another thread.

Executors

It is easy to understand how an application can benefit from spawning an additional thread. Whenever there are independent tasks that can be executed concurrently, spawning more threads to execute them can make the application more efficient. On the other hand, simply spawning more threads does not mean that more tasks can be executed concurrently. On a processor with four cores, spawning ten threads for compute-intensive tasks does not make the application run ten times as fast.

Creating too many threads can, actually, make an application run more slowly. Threads are fairly heavy-weight objects. There is overhead incurred in switching between them. They also impose significant overhead during object allocation and garbage collection. Simply creating new threads haphazardly is not a great strategy.

For a given application running in a particular hardware environment there is an optimum range for the number of threads. Obviously, that number is related to the number of concurrent processes supported by the hardware. It need not, however, be exactly the same.

Applications need a policy for the number of threads they support. As is often the case, the necessary tool is one more layer of abstraction: separating the concept of a task from the thread that happens to execute it. Having already made the mental leap from physical processes (actual concurrency) to threads (unordered execution), this distinction seems nearly obvious. A thread is a virtual process powered by a physical CPU core, and a task is a unit of work. As illustrated in Figure 2.2, tasks are scheduled on threads and threads are scheduled on processors.

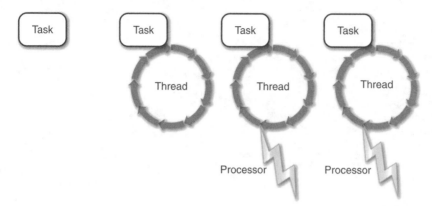

Figure 2.2   Tasks, threads, and processors

The Java concurrency framework, introduced in Java 5, defines a service called an **Executor**. The Executor combines the capability to define a threading policy with the safe publication idiom described in Figure 2.1. An executor is simply a pool of one or more threads servicing a queue of tasks. Tasks are closures, enqueued onto the executor queue in exchange for a **Future**, the promise of a value. Eventually, the task is removed from the queue by one of the executor threads and executed. The result of the execution becomes the value of the future.

Executors are a valuable step up in abstraction from the threads, synchronized blocks, and notifications of the previous section. By using an executor, an application can establish a single, cross-app policy for its optimum number of threads. Most application code simply creates new tasks—small, relatively light-weight objects—and submits them to the executor for asynchronous execution, with minimal concern for overhead and thread safety. An application can, certainly, use more than one Executor. It should be clear, though, that an application with tens of them does not have a threading policy.

Whereas an Executor is an abstraction that separates threading policy from the tasks being executed, an **executor service** is a real-world implementation of the Executor abstraction. It defines messy details like how the executor starts and stops, and whether it is possible to determine which of the two states it is in.

Futures

When one thread, A, requests that another thread, B, asynchronously perform some task on its behalf, there are only a few ways that B can return a result from the task to A. The simplest, of course, is that A can wait for B to complete. That kind of misses the point of concurrency.

Another possibility, popular in web applications, is the callback. Any function

```
f(x1, x2, x3, ..., xn) = y
```

can be transformed into a call

```
f'(x1, x2, x3, ..., xn, g(y))
```

That is, instead of returning a value, as does the function f, f' takes one additional argument, g, which is a function to be called, with the return value. Because the requesting thread, A, has no idea when its method, g, will be called, g commonly enqueues a task to handle the return value on some kind of local queue.

Although this idiom is effective, particularly when the return value is being shipped across a network, it can lead to the infamous "callback hell" in which JavaScript developers all too often find themselves. The method g can be called at multiple and inconvenient times.

Executors use a third strategy, a future. A future is the promise of a value. A client handing a task to an executor receives a future in return. The future is not the value, but the client can treat it as if it were, until it actually needs the value that the future represents. When the client thread cannot make forward progress without the actual value, it is, by definition, prepared to wait for that value. It calls `Future.get`, which suspends the thread until the service thread completes the task and publishes the result into the client thread. This approach drastically reduces the need for callbacks and asynchronous programming.

Summary

This chapter reviewed the essentials of concurrent programming in Java as they will be applied to Android. It established several key features: Thread objects, Java's representation of an asynchronous task, synchronization and monitors, Java's atomicity and visibility constructs, and volatiles, Java's visibility shortcut.

It also introduced a common idiom for safely publishing data from one thread to another and demonstrated its use in the Java Concurrency framework's Executor type. Executors reduce the complexity of current programming by handling many of the aspects of safe publication and enabling an application to establish a parallelization policy, a number of threads that is sufficient to provide optimal parallel execution without incurring excessive scheduling or memory management overhead.

3

The Android Application Model

... the Lord gave, and the Lord has taken away; blessed be the name of the Lord.

JOB 1:21

In the Android environment, the challenge of concurrent programming is compounded by the necessity of dealing with components whose lifecycles are out of the control of the application.

Lifecycles and Components

Android was designed at a time when mobile devices could not reasonably be expected to support paged memory. Whereas most laptops today sport solid-state hard drives, flash memory at the beginning of the century wore out after only approximately 10,000 writes. Using flash memory as swap-space for a general purpose virtual memory system was simply out of the question. In an environment that is limited to only physical memory, an operating system has a hard upper limit on the number of applications that can run at any given time. Android's solution to this problem is to allow the operating system to terminate application process at any time, to recover its memory for another application.

> **Note**
>
> Android's architecture, in which applications are abruptly terminated, is not the only possibility. Early versions of Apple's iOS chose, instead, simply to restrict the number of applications that could be running at any given time.

In an environment in which an app has almost no control over its own lifecycle, the whole idea of an application as an identifiable entity becomes much less meaningful. In the Android world, instead, there are components: **Activities, Services, Providers, and Receivers**. The operating system assures that these components are around when they are needed, spawning a new application process as a side effect, if necessary, to run them.

> ### Note
>
> This description of the Android application model and component lifecycles, in this chapter, depends on some prior familiarity with Android components and their functions. They are not described here. There are many excellent resources that do describe them in great detail. See, for instance:
>
> Griffiths, Dawn and David: *Head First Android Development*, 1st Edition
>
> Mednieks, Dornin, Meike, and Nakamura, *Programming Android*

Whereas the term "application" is roughly synonymous with "process" in many contexts, in Android, an application is simply a collection of coordinating components. A couple of examples will illustrate.

When an Android phone receives a phone call, the system responds, regardless of anything else it might be doing at the time, by showing a page that lets the user pick up the call. To accomplish this, the telephony subsystem sends an **Intent**. The Intent is a small packet of data that describes a required service.

The operating system matches the Intent requirements to a component that supplies those requirements—in this case, an Activity that displays the "Incoming call" page. Note that the requirement expressed in the Intent is not a request to run a particular application. It is a request for a component, in this case a component that can display a page: an Activity. If displaying the Activity necessitates starting an application process, the system does so as a side effect. The goal is to display a page. Starting the application is a means to that end.

A second example is the reverse of the first. When an Android device is booted, the last thing that the system does as it finishes the boot process is to broadcast an Intent (BOOT_COMPLETED) indicating that it is ready to begin normal operation. Components, called Receivers, can register to receive this special broadcast. Every Receiver that is registered for the broadcast receives it shortly after the system boots.

The interesting thing is that some applications contain Receivers that do nothing at all when they receive the broadcast. The applications that contain such Receivers are depending entirely on the side effect. The system starts those applications at boot time, so that it can deliver the Intent to their Receiver components. The application's goal, though, is that it is started every time the system is booted.

The previous examples describe the handling of two different Intents, one starting an Activity in response to a hardware event and the other starting a Receiver in response to a system event. Consider, for a moment, the illustrative lifecycle for a single improbable application that contains both of the sample components, the Activity and the Receiver.

When the system boots, Android attempts to deliver the BOOT_COMPLETED Intent to the application's Receiver. To do that, it must create a process, load the application into the process memory, create an instance of the Receiver object, and then call the Receiver's onReceive method, passing the Intent. Once the onReceive method returns, the Receiver instance is of no further use, is released, and can be garbage collected.

If a phone call comes in soon after the system boots, Android must deliver the call Intent to the application's Activity. It discovers that the application is already running (because of the recently delivered BOOT_COMPLETED Intent), so it needs to only create an instance of the required Activity and run it through its lifecycle.

As illustrated in Figure 3.1, there are now three lifecycles to track: the Receiver, the Activity, and the Application Process.

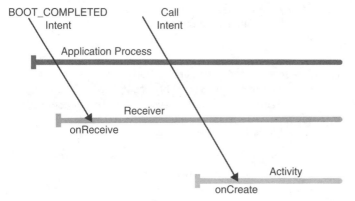

Figure 3.1   Starting an Android process

Process Priority

The lifecycle of the application process might well affect the lifecycles of the two components. Suppose that the system determines that there is insufficient memory available for it to perform some required task. This is unlikely, of course, because the system has just booted. Consider the case, though, just for instructive purposes.

Because it needs memory, the system will review running processes to find the best candidates for termination. It does this by examining the oom_adj attribute for each running process. oom_adj is a small integer whose value is dynamically managed by the system. Smaller values indicate higher process priority (and a smaller chance of process termination): –16 is a very high priority, 15 is very low. Figure 3.2 illustrates.

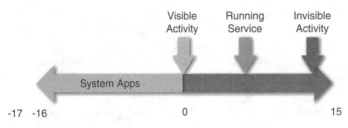

Figure 3.2   OOM-ADJ

> **Note**
>
> It is possible to discover the `oom_adj` of a process running on a device with root access.
>
> Readers comfortable with the command line can use the Android debugger to get access to a shell on a device. The `oom_adj` associated with a given process is cataloged in the file system as the file `/proc/<process-id>/oom-adj`.

Negative (highest priority) numbers are reserved for system applications. If Android ever has to kill its own processes to recover memory, the system is probably about to collapse anyway. The process that contains the Activity currently visible on the device screen has an `oom_adj` of 0. This is the highest priority available for a non-system process. Clearly, it wouldn't make any sense to terminate the process powering the currently visible screen.

A process with no active components (for instance, a process containing only an Activity that is not currently visible) will be given a very high `oom_adj`, making it a likely choice for termination. The important consequence of this is that, immediately upon becoming invisible, an application's chances of being forcefully terminated go from almost nil to very high. Android assumes that the purpose of an Activity component is to power a visible UI page. If the Activity is not displaying a UI page, it is not important and the process powering it can be terminated.

> **Note**
>
> Recent versions of the Linux Kernel, and the versions of Android since KitKat, API level 19 that use those kernels, have replaced `oom_adj` with `oom_score_adj`. `oom_score_adj` is much finer-grained, taking values between 1000 and -1000, lowest priority to highest. Although the numbers have changed, the behavior is essentially the same.

A process with a running Service component has an `oom_adj` that is smaller than that of a process with no active components but greater than that of the process with the visible Activity. A Service component is never as important as the visible Activity, but if it is running, it is more important than an invisible Activity. It is entirely possible, for instance, that some Service component in an application is doing useful work at a time at which none of the application's Activity components is visible. This aspect of service scheduling will play an important part in the application strategy developed in later chapters.

Android terminates an application process by sending it an uncatchable, non-ignorable kill signal (−9). Doing this forces the application process to terminate almost immediately, killing all its threads and de-allocating all its memory. In particular, the components that comprise the application are abruptly terminated.

Although the Android system is free to kill processes as soon as their priority permits, it actually does so fairly lazily. Android memory management, like its close relative, virtual machine garbage collection, does as little work as it can. If there is no immediate need for memory, the effort required to free a process is just a waste of battery.

> **Note**
>
> It is interesting to note that, whereas killing an application with a kill −9 is an extraordinary event on most operating systems, on an Android system it is the most common means of terminating an application.

In the example shown in Figure 3.3, for instance, neither the Receiver nor the Activity have completed their lifecycles yet. Android is being lazy. When their process is killed, however, both are ended abruptly, with prejudice, in mid-lifecycle. There is no warning, no invocation of lifecycle methods, and no goodbye-kiss: just lights out.

The significant consequence of this, of course, is that any state that has not been saved is gone. There is no way to get it back.

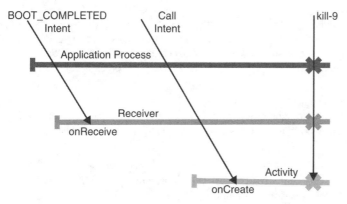

Figure 3.3   Killing an Android process

Component Lifecycles

In an Android application, separate components are entirely separate entities with entirely separate lifecycles. The Android system controls the lifecycles of the components, starting and stopping them as needed.

The canonical example of the lifecycle of an Android component is what happens when a device is rotated. Android's extremely versatile UI system supports completely different screen layouts in portrait and landscape mode. So many things can change when the device is rotated that Android throws away the entire Activity powering the UI in its current configuration and creates a new instance, for the new configuration. Figure 3.4 illustrates what happens in response to screen rotation.

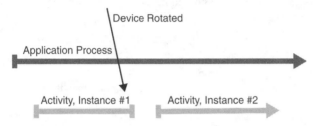

Figure 3.4   Device rotation

The lifecycle of the running instance of the visible Activity is completed. Android calls its onPause, onStop, and onDestroy methods, in that order, and then deletes all references to the Activity. It is now eligible for garbage collection.

> **Note**
>
> Do not confuse process reaping with garbage collection!
>
> Although the two have similar motivations—memory management—process reaping ends the application process, terminating all its threads and de-allocating all its memory. Garbage collection simply recovers unused memory within a process, so that the process can continue running.
>
> The connections between the two kinds of memory management are the onTrimMemory lifecycle events. The Android system uses these events to indicate to an application that there is memory pressure. An application that responds by shrinking is less likely to be killed, to reclaim space.

Component instances come and go even when the task they represent survives. It is easy to imagine that instance #2 of the Activity shown in Figure 3.4 behaves completely identically to its predecessor, instance #1. Nonetheless, instance #1 is gone and forgotten. Instance #2 is the only instance of the Activity in existence. Just as Android creates and destroys processes as it needs them, it creates and destroys instances of components as it needs them.

Again, this has some significant consequences:

- Components that do not save state lose it.
- Code cannot rely on the existence of a component object that it saw even just a moment ago.

Android Applications as Web Apps

Figure 3.5 is another, more complete, portrayal of the lifecycle of an Android application. This time, there are a few more components represented, as well as the user's perception of the application's lifecycle.

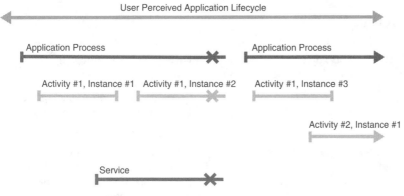

Figure 3.5   Android application lifecycle

It would be intolerable to lose a user's state simply because Android needs memory. Instead, the user expects a continuous, uninterrupted experience. She expects to return to an application in the same state in which she left it, even if that was several days ago. The top line in Figure 3.5, User Perceived Application Lifecycle, models this expectation.

On the other hand, there is no way that an application's process will last for several days. Other applications will come and go, and eventually require memory. The only safe place for state is persistent storage: the file system, the network, and so on.

Web app developers, especially those that worked with J2EE, will probably feel a strong sense of déjà vu looking at Figure 3.5. Android applications are, almost literally, web applications.

Although desktop app developers think a lot about starting and stopping their apps, web-app developers do not. The question of when a web app starts running is nearly meaningless, at least as far as it involves users.

The analogy can be extended. The description of an Activity component as an object with its own lifecycle that is responsible for the workflow of a single UI page, is almost exactly the description of a servlet. Android service components are very similar to J2EE session beans. Even the application bundle, the .apk file, with its manifest, is strongly reminiscent of the .war files used to bundle Java web applications. An Android application is a collection of independent components, declared in a manifest, and run in a container.

> ### Note
> It is even interesting to compare the evolution of Web frameworks with the evolution of Android frameworks. The separation of view, controller, and eventually presenter, improvements in the mechanisms used for queuing network requests, and advancements in testing strategies all have parallels in web app development.

The Android Process

Unless there are specific arrangements to do otherwise, application code will run on one canonical thread. This thread is called the main, or sometimes the UI, thread. Nearly any nontrivial Android application, however, uses multiple threads.

Application Startup

Every Android application is clone of a proto-application called Zygote. A single instance of Zygote is started as part of bringing up the system. It initializes itself, preloading large portions of the Android framework, and then waits for connections to a socket.

When the system needs to create a new application, it connects to the Zygote socket and sends a small packet describing the application to be started. Zygote clones itself, creating a new kernel-level process.

The new process is interesting in that it shares memory with Zygote, its parent, in a mode called **copy-on-write**. Because the two processes use the same memory, starting the child process is almost instantaneous. The kernel does not need to allocate much memory for the new process, nor does the startup need to load the Android framework libraries again. They were all already loaded for Zygote.

Copy-on-write sharing, however, means that if the child application ever tries to change a value in the shared space, the kernel allocates new memory and copies the page into which the child is writing, into it. The new child process can never affect Zygote's memory. Even if the child were to write on every single memory page (and that never happens), the cost of allocating the new memory is amortized over the life of the application, and is not a cost of initialization.

Figure 3.6 shows Zygote's initial memory allocation. Zygote views its memory through a page table which maps memory references into pages of physical memory.

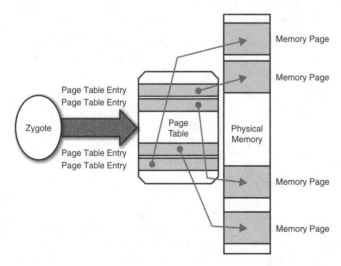

Figure 3.6   Zygote memory

Figure 3.7 shows the creation of a new process for a new application. The new application has its own page table. Most of the new page table is simply a copy of Zygote's page table. It points to the exact same pages of physical memory. Only the pages the new application uses for its own purposes are not shared.

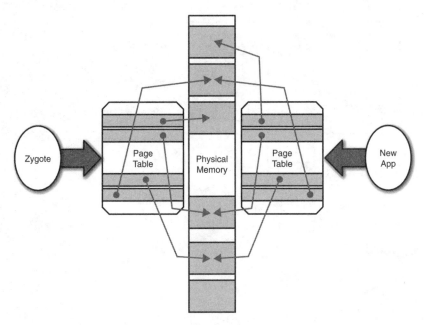

Figure 3.7   A new application shares most of Zygote's memory

Figure 3.8 illustrates what happens when the new application tries to change a memory value. Because the pages are tagged as copy-on-write in the page table, the write attempt triggers a copy. The page is copied over, and the page table is adjusted to point at the new copy. When the write goes through, it modifies only the new application's memory, not Zygote's.

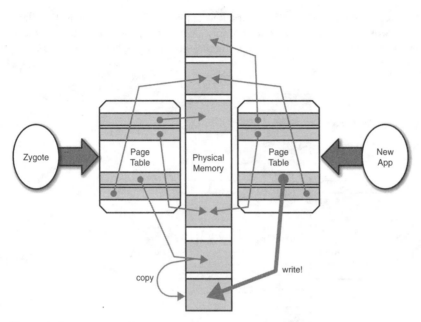

Figure 3.8   Copy-on-write

The Android Main Thread

After a few more initializations—mostly loading the new application into memory—the main thread of the new process initializes itself as a **looper**. A Looper is, essentially, an implementation of the safe publication idiom introduced in Chapter 2, "Java Concurrency."

A thread initialized as a Looper enters a tight loop, servicing a queue. The thread removes the next item from the queue and executes the task it represents. Loopers are discussed in detail in Chapter 5, "Looper/Handler." For now, it is sufficient to understand that the heart of a new Android process is a single thread in a tight loop, processing tasks from a queue.

This thread powers the entire application UI (thus its common name, UI-thread). Many UI methods verify that they are run from the main thread and throw an exception if they are not.

In the early days of the adoption of the model-view-controller (MVC) pattern, developers discovered that it was difficult to build a multithreaded UI that didn't deadlock. The reasons for this are complex, but not all that difficult to grasp, intuitively.

In an MVC architecture, as illustrated in Figure 3.9, one can think of events as flowing in two different directions: from the screen/keyboard, through the Controller, in toward the Model, and then from an updated Model, outward, through the View, to the screen. If there are resources that need to be seized to process in- and outbound events, those resources are likely to be seized in different orders during processing in different directions, making deadlocks nearly inevitable.

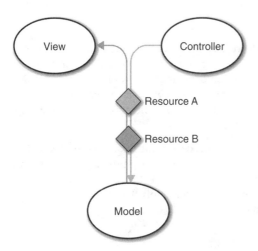

Figure 3.9   Deadlock in the MVC pattern

There are other reasons for making a UI single-threaded. Two important reasons are simplicity and atomicity.

Single-threaded UIs are simple because they run on a single thread. There is no reason to introduce locks, semaphores, synchronization, or thread safety concerns into code that is only run on a single thread. If no more than one thread can ever access object state, then the rule has been satisfied.

A second convenient aspect of a single-threaded UI is that events are atomic. When the main thread removes a task from its queue and begins to execute it, that task has complete control of the UI. If the task involves, for instance, enabling a button on the lower left of the screen, replacing an icon in some view, and repopulating the menu with some new items, there is no possibility that the UI will, because of some kind of race condition, display the new icon and enabled button, but not the menu items. Until the current task is complete, it is in control of all changes made in the UI. Everything that happens between the time it is removed from the queue and the time it releases the thread to process the next task is, from the point of view of the UI, atomic.

Of course, this is also the problem with a single-threaded UI. Android targets a minimum frame rate of 60fps. That means that the main thread needs to process redraw tasks at least every 17ms. That's a lot of CPU time, but not a lot of time for IO, even to the local file system.

So, a major difficulty of building solid, delightful Android programs becomes apparent:

- Application state, displayed through the UI, must be visible to the main thread.

- Application state displayed through the UI must be kept in a persistent store (I/O).

- I/O should not be performed on the main thread. This includes reading and writing files, databases and, of course, the network.

Summary

An Android application is not at all a normal, desktop application. It is much more like a web application: it is built of components that are analogous to the servlets, controllers, and data access layers, familiar to web-devs. The user's perception of an application's lifecycle is related neither to that of the processes that power it nor of the components that comprise it. Android creates and destroys both processes and components when it needs the resources for other purposes.

Android applications are powered, unless the developer makes specific arrangements otherwise, by a single thread, the main thread. This thread is a Looper, a tight loop processing tasks from a queue. It processes each task to completion, before starting the next. This is convenient in that it makes tasks atomic. It can be problematic, though. When a task involves I/O or, for some other reason takes a long time to complete, it stalls the user-visible UI.

4

Async Tasks and Loaders

Try to understand what the author wished to do, and do not blame him for not achieving what he did not attempt.

John Updike, Picked-Up Pieces

The *AsyncTask* is the first Android concurrency tool to which most developers are introduced when learning the platform. It is a clever and powerful tool for certain kinds of jobs. Unfortunately, developers who have not yet discovered any other tools frequently apply it in situations for which it is completely inappropriate. Community knowledge of best practices for using AsyncTasks—and even some prejudice against using it at all—become more firmly established and more broadly distributed than they were even five years ago. Still, including the word "thread" in a question posted to the StackOverflow Android group will almost certainly cause at least one response that describes a solution involving an AsyncTask—whether it is appropriate or not.

Async Task Architecture

Conceptually, an AsyncTask is pretty simple. It is just a way to execute a segment of code on another thread. Consider Listing 4.1.

Listing 4.1 **A Database Query**

```
// Things that happen before the db query…

Cursor c = getContentResolver().query(
    DataProvider.URI,
    REQ_COLS,
    COL_LAST_NAME + "=?",
```

```
        new String[] { userName },
        COL_LAST_NAME + " ASC" );

// Things that happen after the db query...
```

The code, though perhaps a little ugly, is completely correct and already does exactly what it should. The only problem is that because the database query might easily take many milliseconds, it should not be executed on the main thread. The necessary change appears so minor and so unrelated to the job of getting data from the database that it seems as though it should be possible to accomplish it with an equally minor change in the code. It would be wonderful if, in some idealized computer language, it were possible to write something like the code shown in Listing 4.2.

Listing 4.2 **Idealistic Backgrounding**

```
// Things that happen before the db query...

Cursor c;
inBackground {
    c = getContentResolver().query(
        DataProvider.URI,
        REQ_COLS,
        COL_LAST_NAME + "=?",
        new String[] { userName },
        COL_LAST_NAME + " ASC");
}

// Things that happen after the db query...
```

Sadly, there is no `inBackground` keyword in Java.

The idea though, is not at all unreasonable. Some languages (Swift and Scala, to name two) support constructs that look a lot like this. In those languages, the block of code following `inBackground` is wrapped in a language construct called a **closure**.

Java 8 supports closures with its new lambda expression syntax. As of the, currently un-named, Android N, Android's Java will support them too. Suppose that Listing 4.2 were code that could be compiled by some future Android compiler. Can closures actually solve the problem? Are they sufficient?

In languages that support closures, `inBackground` need not be a keyword. Instead, it could be a call to a method that takes a single argument—a closure—and executes that closure on a different thread. Listing 4.2 might be rewritten as shown in Listing 4.3.

Listing 4.3 **Passing a Closure to a Function**

```
// Things that happen before the db query…

inBackground(
    closure (localUserName = userName) {
        getContentResolver().query(
            DataProvider.URI,
            REQ_COLS,
            COL_LAST_NAME + "=?",
            new String[] { localUserName },
            COL_LAST_NAME + " ASC" );
    });

// State of the query is undefined, here…
```

Clearly, this is still not Java. The argument to the `inBackground` method is, roughly, a reference to a block of code, not the result of executing it. In the listing, this is represented by the invented keyword `closure`.

The `inBackground` method runs the closure on another thread. In particular, one can imagine that it uses exactly the safe publication pattern described in Chapter 3, "The Android Application Model." It would push the closure onto a queue from which it would be retrieved for execution by a background thread.

There are, however, several loose ends. There are restrictions on the code inside the closure (the enclosed code) that are necessary to make it behave exactly as the corresponding code did in Listing 4.1.

First (at least in this imaginary language), the code inside the closure cannot use the keywords `return`, `break`, or `continue`. Inside the closure those keywords have a very different meaning than they do outside it. If Listing 4.1 contained a `return` statement, for instance, executing it would return control to the caller. If that same `return` statement were wrapped in a closure and executed on a background thread it almost certainly could not do the same thing.

Another restriction is that if the code in the closure throws an exception, that exception will not abruptly terminate the code that calls the `inBackground` method. Just as in the case of the `return` statement, if the postulated `inBackground` method runs the closure on a different thread, the exception will unwind the background thread stack, not that of the calling thread.

A more onerous restriction is that any preconditions like variables and so on that are used in the enclosed code must have their values available from within the closure. If the closure is to behave, when executed at a completely different time and in a completely different environment, as it would have had it been executed in place, all the variables used within it must have the values they would have had when the closure was created.

Assuming normal Java naming conventions, the only symbol in the enclosed code that does not represent a constant is `userName`. Listing 4.3 postulates using the invented `closure` keyword to assign its value to a new local constant, `localUserName`. Obviously, things would be wildly more complex if the enclosed code referred to lots of variables, assigned any of them, or worse yet, depended on side effects in the surrounding code.

Anyone who has done any significant amount of Java development will realize that it is possible to do something similar in Java, using an anonymous class. The example from Listing 4.3 might be rewritten in compilable Java, as shown in Listing 4.4.

Listing 4.4   **A Database Query**

```
// Things that happen before the query…

final String localUserName = userName;

inBackground(
    new Runnable () {
        @Override public void run() {
            getContentResolver().query(
                DataProvider.URI,
                REQ_COLS,
                COL_LAST_NAME + "=?",
                new String[]{localUserName},
                COL_LAST_NAME + " ASC");
        } });

// State of the query is undefined, here…
```

Since its creation, Java has always been able to emulate closure-like behavior. It is just that its expression is verbose and, as this example demonstrates, fairly restrictive.

The restrictions are beginning to mount up, too. This attempt at expressing in code something that is so easy to say: "just run this fragment on a different thread," turns out to be fairly difficult. Closures, even in their historical implementation as anonymous classes are, without doubt, useful tools. It is already clear, though, that they will not support the ideal of a simple construct that executes arbitrary code, unmodified, on another thread.

There is one more issue. While left for last, it is the most obvious and troublesome. Somehow, the post-conditions—the changes in state resulting from the execution of the enclosed code—must be returned to the caller. In the example, the cursor, c, must be available to the code that follows the call to inBackground.

The whole point of this exercise has been to get a segment of code executed asynchronously. The most obvious direct consequence is that the enclosed code will no longer be executed strictly before the first line of code after the closure block. Suddenly the code that used to happen after the query and thus after the cursor had been obtained no longer does so.

The AsyncTask provides a solution to this problem.

> **Note**
>
> The fact that Java 8 closures have been introduced into Android Java in the version called "N", at the time of this writing, does not affect this discussion at all. Whether represented as anonymous classes, or implemented with the new `invokedynamic` instruction closures are, for all of the reasons cited here, insufficient, alone, for moving a block of code to another thread.

Async Task Basics

At its heart, an AsyncTask is just an extension of the scheme from the previous section, warts and all. Inspired by Java's SwingWorker, it has the same goal as the previous examples—moving a segment of code to a background thread—and all the same constraints. Its sole purpose is to run a code segment on a background thread. Ideally the code segment would just be cut from its current location, pasted into the task, and the cut code replaced by a call that executes the task.

Architecturally, the `AsyncTask` class is the realization of a classic design pattern, the type-safe template. Its definition has one abstract method, the template method `doInBackground`. As is typical with the template pattern, the `AsyncTask` class is abstract, and the only way to use it is to create a subclass. To execute code on a background thread, create a subclass of `AsyncTask` and paste the code into the implementation of the `doInBackground` method in the subclass.

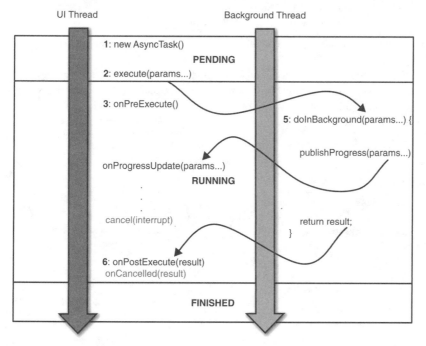

Figure 4.1   Async task

Code encapsulated in an AsyncTask is executed in the steps illustrated in Figure 4.1:

1. Create a new instance of the task. A task instance can be used only once. An attempt to run it a second time will cause it to throw an `IllegalStateException`.

2. Call the new instance's `execute` method, passing parameters.

3. The task's `onPreExecute` method is invoked on the caller's thread. If there is setup common to all executions of the task, that setup belongs in the subclass's implementation of `onPreExecute`.

4. The task's `doInBackground` method is scheduled on an executor. The arguments passed to the task's `execute` method (in step #1) are published into the executor thread and become the parameters to `doInBackground`.

5. The `doInBackground` method executes and completes. During its execution, a call to the task's `cancel` method will mark the task as cancelled. Only a flag, cancellation does not necessarily interrupt the task or cause to terminate immediately. An exception, thrown in the `doInBackground` method will, however, terminate the entire task abruptly. None of the subsequent steps are executed.

6. One of the two completion methods is scheduled on the main thread. If the task's `cancel` method was called at any time before the task resumes on the main thread, its `onCancel` method is called, with the return value from `doInBackground`. If `cancel` was not called, `onPostExecute` is called with the return value instead.

7. The task is now complete and should be released so that it can be garbage collected.

As the preceding exercise illustrated, the code to be executed on the background thread must have its environment passed to it and must be able to return the results of its computations. The `AsyncTask` class makes this explicit by using the parameters and return value of the `doInBackground` method. It uses Java generics to make these values type-safe.

Listing 4.5 shows the code from Listing 4.1 implemented as an AsyncTask.

Listing 4.5 **A Simple Async Task**

```
private class GetNamesTask extends AsyncTask<String, Void, Cursor> {
    @Override protected Cursor doInBackground(String… userName) {
        return getContentResolver().query(
            DataProvider.URI,
            REQ_COLS,
            COL_LAST_NAME + "=?",
            new String[] { userName[0] },
            COL_LAST_NAME + " ASC");
    }

    @Override
    public onPostExecute(Cursor cursor) {
        onCursorReceived(cursor);
    }
}
```

The first generic parameter to the abstract `AsyncTask` class (`String` in Listing 4.5) is the type of the parameters to `execute` and also to `doInBackground`. This is the environment passed into the enclosed code.

> ### Note
>
> The AsyncTask `execute` method uses Java **varargs**. It accepts multiple arguments and passes them, eventually, to `doInBackground` as an array. The first argument to `execute`, for example, is `param[0]` in `doInBackground`, the second is `param[1]`, and so on.
>
> For example, a subclass of AsyncTask defined like this:
>
> ```
> class SomeTask extends AsyncTask<Uri, Void, Void>
> ```
> might be called like this:
> ```
> new SomeTask.execute(
>     Uri.parse("content://sample.com/table1")
>     Uri.parse("content://sample.com/table2"));
> ```
> In which case, within the `doInBackground` method, declared as:
> ```
>     public void doInBackground(Uri… uris)
> ```
> `uris[0]` is the uri `content://sample.com/table1`, and `uris[1]` is the uri `content://sample.com/table2`.
>
> The only constraint is that all the arguments must be of the parameter type or one of its subtypes. Attempting to call the execute method, like this, for instance:
> ```
> new SomeTask.execute(
>     "content://sample.com/table1"
>     Uri.parse("content://sample.com/table2"));
> ```
> … with one String and one Uri, would cause a compiler error.

Listing 4.5 also demonstrates the AsyncTask solution to the problem of delivering the results of the background computation back to the calling code. The return from the call to `doInBackground` is delivered to another method, `onPostExecute`. `onPostExecute` runs on the main thread and is guaranteed to execute only after `doInBackground` completes. At last, there is a place to put code that can be executed, only after the background code has run. The third generic argument (`Cursor` in Listing 4.5) is the type of the value returned by `doInBackground` and therefore, the type of the parameter to `onPostExecute`.

> ### Note
>
> The second generic parameter to AsyncTask controls the type of the parameters to a progress-reporting feature implemented by the two methods `publishProgress` (called on the worker thread, by implementation code, from within `doInBackground`) and `onProgressUpdate` (called back on the main thread, in response).
>
> This mechanism is nifty, but does not materially affect the behavior of the AsyncTask and thus is not discussed here. It is described in the documentation at http://developer.android.com/reference/android/os/AsyncTask.html.

Listing 4.6 **Executing an AsyncTask**

```
    // Things that happen before the db query...

    new GetNamesTask().execute(userName);

    // ...
}

void onCursorReceived(Cursor cursor) {
    // Things that happen after the db query...
}
```

The code that originally followed the database query in program order is now in a new method that is called from the task. Previously, program order guaranteed that this code was executed after the query. Now the AsyncTask contract guarantees it.

AsyncTask Execution

The precise implementation of AsyncTask has changed over time. Reviewing the actual code, though, both present and historical, reveals facts that are at odds with the official documentation.

The documentation claims that the AsyncTask mechanism was single-threaded, until API level 4, Donut. It seems entirely plausible that in very old versions of Android, AsyncTask (like its close relative, AsyncQueryHandler), ran on a single background thread. As early as API level 3, Cupcake, however, they were executed as they are now, on a Java thread-pool executor, the THREAD_POOL_EXECUTOR. Until fairly recently, regardless of the device, this executor used between 1 and 10 threads.

This strategy changed significantly in 2011, near the release of API Level 11, Honeycomb. Instead of submitting tasks directly to the executor, where they might be executed out of order, a new implementation of AsyncTask introduced a new executor, the SERIAL_EXECUTOR. This new executor is simply the old executor with a queue in front of it. Tasks submitted to the SERIAL_EXECUTOR for execution are pushed onto the queue, where they wait until previously submitted tasks have completed execution. When a task's turn arrives, it is executed on an executor that is, essentially, identical to that used in Cupcake. Because of the queue, though, tasks are executed in submission order and each runs to completion before the next begins.

Without a doubt, this change was made, as the Android documentation says, "… to avoid common application errors caused by parallel execution" (http://developer.android.com/reference/android/os/AsyncTask.html). One can imagine a developer tearing his hair out over a seldom-occurring crash caused by an attempt to store something in a database that did not yet exist, or write to a file that was not yet open. That is now less likely to happen.

On the other hand, AsyncTasks are no longer executed concurrently! There is, however, a way to return to parallel execution. At the same time that normal AsyncTask execution was serialized, the framework introduced a new method, executeOnExecutor. The new method's first argument is the executor to which the AsyncTask is to be submitted. Because the bare thread-pool executor `THREAD_POOL_EXECUTOR` is a public constant in the `AsyncTask` class, developers who are certain that they want parallel execution can bypass the queue by calling:

```
task.executeOnExecutor(AsyncTask.THREAD_POOL_EXECUTOR,…)
```

Note that with this method, it is also possible to enqueue AsyncTasks onto application-specific executors. For example, developers who find the serial execution model of the default AsyncTask appealing but who have to accommodate the occasional long-running background task that blocks the timely execution of all other tasks, might consider creating a third executor, the `LARGE_TASK_EXECUTOR`, strictly for the parallel execution of slower tasks. This kind of architecture—creating a tiered priority scheme for different types of tasks—can be quite effective.

The fact that the tasks are now run in order does not imply that they are all run on a single thread! This is the second deviation from the official documentation. It is absolutely possible that the executor uses only a single thread for all tasks. As mentioned earlier, versions of Android prior to API Level 19 initialized the AsyncTask executor thread pool with a single thread. If, either by chance or because of the queue, only one task at a time is ever presented to the executor, it might never grow its pool beyond that single thread. In that case, the single thread would run all the tasks.

In 2013, though, for API Level 19, KitKat, the core size of the thread pool was changed to be the number of CPUs plus one. The maximum size of the pool was changed to be twice the number of CPUs, plus one. The executor's thread pool, since then, is likely to have at least two threads and can have more.

This is significant because it means that `doInBackground` methods of AsyncTasks cannot safely communicate without synchronization. Listing 4.7 would be correct if there were a guarantee that all `doInBackground` methods ran on the same thread. Because there is no such guarantee, the code is not correct.

Listing 4.7 **Incorrect Cross-Task Communication**

```
static boolean mFlag;

private class IncorrectTask extends AsyncTask<Void, Void, Void> {
    @Override protected Void doInBackground(Void… empty) {
        if (!mFlag) { // !!! Incorrect
            mFlag = true;
            // …
        }
        // …
        return null;
    }
}
```

AsyncTask Completion

The AsyncTask framework does not support exceptions thrown from within the doInBackground method. If the code in doInBackground terminates abruptly, the entire task lifecycle is also terminated abruptly, and neither onPostExecute, nor onCancelled is called. This is almost certainly a program error. The doInBackground method should always exit normally.

When doInBackground finishes, the AsyncTask framework completes the task lifecycle by scheduling the execution of exactly one of the two methods, onCancelled or onPostExecute, back on the main thread. Normally, it is the latter method, onPostExecute, that is called. If, however, the task's cancel method is called between the time the task is started (with the call to its execute method) and the time the framework decides which of the two completion methods to call, the onCancelled method is called instead.

Note that the AsyncTask contract does not promise that the completion methods onPostExecute or onCancelled will be run on the thread from which the execute method was called. It promises only that that method will be run on the *main* thread. If execute is called from some other thread—for instance, in the doInBackground method of some other AsyncTask—onPreExecute will be called on the same thread as that on which execute was invoked. The onPostExecute method, however, will run on the main thread. The normal assumption that onPreExecute and onPostExecute are run on the same thread is not valid in this case and all rules about concurrent access to mutable state apply.

A call to a task's onCancelled method is not evidence that the doInBackground method observed a call to the cancel method. There are several ways that onCancelled might be called even after doInBackground completes normally. The simplest of these is that the call to cancel occurs between the completion of doInBackground and the time that the completion method is scheduled, back on the main thread.

Another possibility, though, occurs because the cancel method is extremely polite. The default implementation does very little to force the doInBackground method to abort. It simply sets a flag that says the task has been cancelled and, if the boolean argument to cancel was set true, uses Java's thread interruption mechanism to request that the thread running the task stop doing so. It is up to the implementation of doInBackground to notice this request and to act on it.

If the task is waiting for the completion of a blocking operation, when cancel is called with its argument set true, the thread will be interrupted and the operation aborted. Most I/O operations and all the low-level thread-blocking operations terminate abruptly with an exception when interrupted. I/O operations throw an InterruptedIOException, and thread-blocking operations throw an InterruptedException. In either case, a correctly written doInBackground method must catch the exception and return some partial value or failure flag. Of course, a task that enables itself to be interrupted with cancel(true) must also gracefully handle thread interrupts even when they happen elsewhere, when the code is not blocked.

If, on the other hand, the computation in doInBackground is CPU bound—perhaps translating a bitmap or computing the value of π to a million digits—it must periodically check to see whether it has been interrupted. This check is accomplished with a call to the AsyncTask method isCancelled.

> **Note**
>
> Don't swallow interrupts!
>
> Interrupting a thread sets a flag in the `Thread` object. The `Thread.interrupted` method returns the value of that flag *and clears it!* Most of the blocking operations that terminate abruptly in response to interruption also clear the flag before they throw. The `Thread.currentThread().isInterrupted` method is the only way of discovering the interrupted state without changing it.
>
> When designing interruptible tasks, the state of the interrupt flag is a part of the API. If callers need to be aware of an interruption, be sure to reset the flag, using the `Thread.currentThread().interrupt` method, after using `Thread.interrupted` to test its state, or catching an interruption exception.

Making the `doInBackground` method cancellable can be a significant challenge and might require adaptations in architecture far from the task itself. Consider Listing 4.8, a task that is very similar to those in the previous examples.

Listing 4.8   **Incorrect Cross-Task Communication**

```
private class DbInsert extends AsyncTask<ContentValues, Void, Integer> {
    @Override protected Void doInBackground(ContentValues… values) {
        return Integer.valueOf(
            getContentResolver().bulkInsert(DataProvider.URI, values))
    }
}
```

Instead of a query, this task is doing a potentially large insert. It is entirely possible that it will take several seconds to complete. Sadly, SQLite operations are not interruptible. Most of the implementation of SQLite is portable C code. It pays no attention at all to Java's thread interruption flag.

Is it even possible, then, to make this task cancellable? Under some circumstances, it is possible. Making the task cancellable in this case, for instance, might be accomplished with changes to the architecture of the provider. The example is instructive.

Remember that the call to `ContentResolver.bulkInsert` is proxied to whichever content provider has authority for the URL: `DataProvider.URI`. The call to `ContentResolver.bulkInsert` is handled by that provider's `bulkInsert` method. If the AsyncTask in Listing 4.8 is to be interruptible, it is that method that must support interruption. Listing 4.9 demonstrates this.

Listing 4.9   **Interruptable Bulk Insert**

```
@Override
public int bulkInsert(Uri uri, ContentValues[] rows) {
    SQLiteDatabase db = getDb();
    db.beginTransaction();
    try {
        int inserted = 0;
```

```
        for (int len = rows.length; inserted < len; inserted++) {
            db.insert(Db.TABLE, null, rows[inserted]);
            if (Thread.interrupted()) { break; }  // not recommended :-(
        }
        db.setTransactionSuccessful();
    }
    finally { db.endTransaction(); }
    return inserted;
}
```

This kind of trick is fragile and definitely *not recommended*. It works, for instance, only if the bulkInsert method runs on the same background thread as the doInBackground method. If, as is sometimes the case, the content provider is running in a separate process, it will not observe or honor the interruption. A much better solution would have DbInsert chunk the records into multiple, separate insert calls to the provider, and to check the isCancelled method between those calls.

Making an AsyncTask cancellable can depend on making the best of code over which the designer of the task itself has no control.

Using AsyncTasks

Armed with an understanding of the implementation of the AsyncTask, let's turn to exploring how to use them effectively in applications. Such a simple tool! What could possibly go wrong?

AsyncTask: Considered Dangerous

Sadly, there are just so many things that can go wrong. Errors with AsyncTasks fall into two categories: concurrency errors and lifecycle errors.

Getting It Wrong: Concurrency

Concurrency errors are simple violations of Java concurrency rules. Listing 4.10 is an example.

Listing 4.10 **AsyncTask with a Concurrency Error**

```
@Override
public void onClick(View v) {
    new AsyncTask<Void, Void, Void>() {
        @Override
        protected Void doInBackground(Void... args) {
            String msg = textView.getText(); // !!!
            textView.setText("");             // !!!
            network.post(msg);
            return null;
        }
    }.execute();
}
```

The whole point of the doInBackground method is that it runs on a different thread! The observant reader will notice that the call to textView.getText is an unsynchronized reference to an object visible to another thread (in this case a View object owned by the main thread). This code is incorrect.

Fortunately, this code will fail in a very obvious way at runtime. Many of the methods in the Android view framework verify that they are called from the main thread and fail if they are not. The call to setText in this AsyncTask will generate a ViewRootImpl$CalledFromWrong ThreadException. Note, though, that the call to getText is equally incorrect but does not generate an exception.

Static analysis tools, discussed in Chapter 8, "Concurrency Tools," might be able to identify issues like this, before runtime. Among such tools, recent versions of Android Studio support the new Android annotations @UiThread, @MainThread, @WorkerThread and @BinderThread. These annotations, applied to methods, help static analysis tools report incorrect code.

Listing 4.10 demonstrates the concurrency issues that can arise from references to in-scope variables from within the doInBackground method. Listing 4.11 shows a related problem.

Listing 4.11 **Another AsyncTask with a Concurrency Error**

```
@Override
public void onClick(View v) {
    new AsyncTask<TextView, Void, Void>() {
        @Override
        protected Void doInBackground(TextView... args) {
            TextView view = args[0];
            String msg = view.getText(); // !!!
            view.setText("");            // !!!
            network.post(msg);
            return null;
        }
    }.execute(textView);
}
```

Passing the mutable value into doInBackground as a parameter does not help! In fact, it just makes the problem a little more difficult to spot. The local variable view, the method parameter args[0] and the class member textView all refer to exactly the same object. Because those references are visible from multiple threads, the code is incorrect.

Listing 4.11 will fail, dramatically, at runtime, exactly as did the code in Listing 4.10. Listing 4.12 illustrates the same problem yet one more time, but in a way that will fail in a much less predictable manner.

Listing 4.12 **Yet Another AsyncTask with a Concurrency Error**

```
@Override
public void updateHandler(List<String> strings) {
    new AsyncTask<List<String>, Void, Void>() {
        @Override
        protected Void doInBackground(List<String>... args) {
            List<String> s = args[0]
            for (int i = 0, n = s.size(), i < n; i++) {
                network.post(s.get(i));
            }
            return null;
        }
    }.execute(strings);
}
```

The problem here is that once again the code is leaking references to a mutable object into the worker thread. The parameter to `updateHandler`, `strings`, is aliased, inside `doInBackground` as `args[0]` and `s`. Because `strings` is a reference to a mutable data structure passed to `updateHandler` as a parameter, it is impossible to know how many other references are being used, elsewhere in the program.

> **Note**
>
> `Collections.unmodifilable` is not a solution.
>
> Wrapping a mutable object in an immutable view does not solve the problem. The Java Collections Library method `Collections.unmodifiableList`, for example, simply creates an unmodifiable view of the list. Unless all references to a list are wrapped, with the unmodifiable wrapper, the thread on which the `doInBackground` method runs still holds a reference to an object that can be modified from another thread.

The only way to make this code correct is, as Listing 4.13 demonstrates, to make local copies of all mutable data structures. In this case, that simply means copying the list. If the elements of the list were mutable, they would have to be copied, too.

Listing 4.13 **A Less-Broken AsyncTask**

```
@Override
public void updateHandler(List<String> strings) {
    new AsyncTask<List<String>, Void, Void>() {
        @Override
        @WorkerThread
        protected Void doInBackground(List<String>... args) {
            List<String> s = args[0];
            for (int i = 0, n = s.size(), i < n; i++) {
                network.post(s.get(i));
            }
        }
    }
}
```

```
            return null;
        }
    }.execute(new ArrayList(strings));
}
```

To summarize, the problem is that Java's block structure and threading structure don't always play nicely together. Things that happen automatically are sometimes very dangerous. Just getting concurrency right in an AsyncTask requires attention to detail.

... And concurrency is not the end of it.

Getting It Wrong: Lifecycles

Among the most common errors in using AsyncTasks are those that relate to Android component lifecycles. Listings 4.14 and 4.15 are perfect examples of this kind of error. Both are trying to post data to the network in response to user input. Consider, for a moment, how this code might fail.

Suppose a user installs the app containing this code on his phone and, just by chance, invokes that AsyncTask just as the subway train he is riding goes underground and loses connectivity. Without connectivity, the post request will, eventually, time out.

A reasonable choice of timeout interval might be something like 60 seconds. Although many mobile applications choose much smaller numbers (10 to 15 seconds) for actions for which a user must wait, 30 to 90 seconds might make sense for a task performed asynchronously.

When a connection times out, it is typically retried, perhaps with some kind of back-off algorithm. The post method in Listing 4.12 might, for instance, retry after 30 seconds, 90 seconds and, finally at 180 seconds. The task is working away for a full 3 minutes after the user took the action that started it.

Recall Figure 3.4 from Chapter 3. It showed the lifecycle of an activity and how it related to the user's perception of the application's lifecycle. Figure 4.2 shows that same lifecycle but adds an AsyncTask, spawned by the activity.

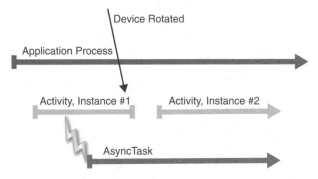

Figure 4.2   AsyncTask lifecycle

The Android framework controls the lifecycle of the Activity. There are many reasons—screen rotation is the most often cited—that the framework might decide to discard one instance of an Activity, and replace it with another instance at a later time.

The lifecycle of the AsyncTask, however, is not managed at all. Figure 4.2 illustrated the example under consideration, in which the task is around for several minutes after the Activity that spawned it is gone. Clouds are beginning to gather.

To understand exactly why this is a problem, consider first a slight refactoring of the example code. In Listing 4.14, the task is promoted to the named inner class `PostTask`, instead of the anonymous class used previously. In particular, note that in its constructor, `PostTask` takes a `Context` as an argument and retains a reference to it in the networking object that it creates. The Context passed into `PostTask` is the current Activity.

Figure 4.3 illustrates the resulting problem.

Listing 4.14 **AsyncTask with a Lifecycle Error**

```
private static class PostTask extends AsyncTask<String, Void, Void>() {
    private final Network network;

    public PostTask(Context ctxt) { this.network = new Network(ctxt); }

    @Override
    protected Void doInBackground(String... args) {
        network.post(args[0]);
        return null;
    }
}

    // …
    public void onClick(View v) {
        view.setText("");
        new PostTask(this).execute(textView.getText().toString());
    }
```

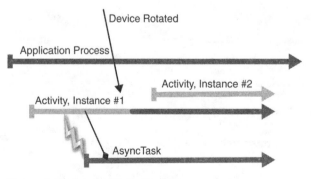

Figure 4.3 A leaked AsyncTask

Because the task holds a reference to the Activity, the Activity cannot be garbage collected, even after the Android framework has created its replacement. As shown in Figure 4.3, the AsyncTask hangs around for several minutes. During those several minutes, the redundant Activity, a very large object, and most of the objects to which it refers—perhaps an entire redundant view hierarchy—are stuck in memory.

Notice that all implementations of AsyncTasks as non-static inner classes—and this includes all anonymous classes—have this problem! In Java, any non-static class B defined within another class A holds a reference to the instance of A that created it. The two classes B1 and B2, for instance, in Listing 4.15, have nearly identical implementations.

Listing 4.15   **Inner Class Implementation**

```
class A {
    private class B1 { }

    private static class B2 {
        private A parent;
        public B2(A parent) { this.parent = parent }
    }
}
```

Every anonymous subclass of AsyncTask holds the Activity that created it in memory until the task completes.

There is another reason that the zombie Activity is a problem: The task might actually try to use the reference that it is holding. On noticing that an the AsyncTask.onPostExecute method is run on the main thread, a developer can be forgiven for thinking she's found a perfect way to notify the user of a task's completion. She simply stores a reference to a notification view in the task, and updates it in onPostExecute.

Figure 4.3 illustrates why this doesn't work. At the very best, the onPostExecute method updates a zombie view that is no longer attached to the screen. At worst, because the Activity has been run through the end of its lifecycle and its onDestroy method called, it is in an inconsistent state and throws an exception, crashing the application.

Weak references are often suggested as a solution to this problem. Experienced Java developers will recall that the Java runtime regards an object as garbage when there are no strong references to it. Nearly all references in Java are strong: objects are never garbage as long as there are variables that point to them.

A WeakReference is a special Java object. It contains a reference to a single other Java object. One might think of it as a list that can have only one thing in it. It is special because the object to which it refers *can* be garbage collected. If all the remaining references to an object are weak references, the object is garbage collected and all the weak reference are set to null.

If an AsyncTask holds only weak references to its Activity, then it is impossible for it to create a zombie. When all framework references—hard references—to the Activity are gone, it will be garbage collected. At some later time, when the AsyncTask attempts to refer to the Activity, it simply checks, finds that the reference to it is null, and takes appropriate action. This certainly seems like a silver bullet. It is not and there are three reasons why.

> **Note**
>
> AsyncTasks are almost never the right choice for network operations.
>
> This might seem like a strong statement. There are many applications in the App Store, some perhaps with 4- and 5-star ratings, that have networking architectures that depend on AsyncTasks.
>
> ... And the Leaning Tower of Pisa is still upright, mostly. Choosing a better architecture for network operations will mean less erratic behavior and will give you more time to focus on delighting your users.

The most obvious reason is that the task might need to take action and might be unable to do so. In the previous sample scenario, three minutes after the user believes she has posted something to the network, the post fails. If the AsyncTask cannot report the failure, the application is breaking promises. The user's post was not sent, and there is no longer any reliable way of informing her that it failed.

The second reason is the cost. Consider an AsyncTask that does something fairly complex: perhaps making calls to two or more REST services and computing some kind of aggregation of the data it receives. Now consider what happens if this task loses its Activity early in its lifecycle. It proceeds to make each expensive network transfer and then heats up the CPU calculating the aggregate and, finally *throws the result away*. The data transfer can cost the user real money. The calculation certainly costs real battery life. When the work is done, however, there is no place to put the result, so it is just discarded. What a waste!

The final reason that using weak references to embed AsyncTasks in Activities is bad design is that it is, well, bad design. The entire concern about zombie activities is not really a problem to be solved, but rather an artifact of a bad architecture. Long running asynchronous tasks do not belong in Activities at all. Activities are meant to be short-lived objects. Chapter 3 compared them to servlets. No one would put business logic into a servlet. Chapter 3 also noted that a process that contains only Activities that are not visible is eligible for process reaping. An AsyncTask running in an application that contains only an invisible Activity can be killed, mid-process, with no warning and no chance to report failure.

Android applications, like their three-tier web-service counterparts, should put substantial asynchronous work into a more appropriate component. In Android, that component is usually a Service. Services are the subject of Chapter 6, "Services, Processes, and IPC."

Getting It Right

At this point the reader can be forgiven for thinking that AsyncTasks are an abomination that should never be used at all. This reactionary opinion is not unheard of within the Android developer community. Discussions among Android developers with an app or two under their belts often include a tacit, unspecific assumption that AsyncTasks are something that the cat dragged in.

As is so often the case in software development, it is the specific details that make the difference. AsyncTasks are not a panacea. Neither, however, are they useless. Understanding them, when they are useful and when they are not, will be very helpful in assessing the next new hotness when it arrives.

AsyncTasks have their place. Here are a couple of recipes for building ones that are resilient and useful.

Autonomous Tasks

To qualify as autonomous, an AsyncTask must have only side effects: it must not try to resynchonize and return information—even status—to the caller. It should also be relatively short-running—no more than a few seconds.

Such a task can be very useful for accomplishing something that is either very likely to succeed or that can be tested and retried if it fails. Creating and initializing a file, for instance, is appropriate work for this kind of task. If the application needs the file and it does not exist, it starts a task to create it. At some future time, when it discovers again that it needs the file, the file is probably there. If not, it just starts another task.

Cancellable Tasks

A cancellable task is one that actually responds to the `cancel` method by ceasing processing. Such a task terminates its `doInBackground` method as quickly as possible, and exits, upon receiving cancellation notification. When the executor releases it and it finishes its lifecycle, it is garbage collected and cannot cause the retention of objects to which it holds references.

Of course, a cancellable task needs to be cancelled! When an Activity starts a cancellable AsyncTask, it must remember it and then cancel it, typically in response to `onPause` or `onStop` events.

Loaders and Cursor Loaders

The `CursorLoader` is a nearly ideal example of an appropriate use of an AsyncTask. Its base class, `Loader`, is an abstraction of asynchronous data loading. The subclass `AsyncTaskLoader` is an implementation of the abstraction as an `AsyncTask`. `CursorLoader`, a subclass of `AsyncTaskLoader` is perhaps the best answer to the problem that begins this chapter: asynchronously loading a cursor full of data from a database.

Mark Murphy, author of "The Busy Coder's Guide to Android Development" (2009) once called Loaders "a failed abstraction." This is an accurate assessment. Loaders just haven't caught on as the generic solution for loading data into a view. Although not successful as a generalized abstraction, the specific derived class `CursorLoader` is a solid and popular tool.

The goal when using a CursorLoader is to get the data from the database. The solution at first seems like the long way around the barn. It is a three-step process that seems to start off in the wrong direction entirely:

1. Ask the loader manager to create a loader.

2. Give the loader manager a loader when it asks for it.

3. Accept the cursor returned by the loader when it is delivered.

Consider an application that will display the results of a database query in a list view. The skeleton Activity might look something like Listing 4.16.

Listing 4.16   **Skeleton Cursor List Activity**

```
public class LoaderActivity extends ListActivity {

    // ...

    @Override
    protected void onCreate(Bundle state) {
        super.onCreate(state);

        SimpleCursorAdapter adapter = new SimpleCursorAdapter(
            this,
            R.layout.list_row,
            null,
            FROM,
            TO,
            0);

        setListAdapter(adapter);
    }

    // ...

}
```

The third argument to the `SimpleCursorAdapter` constructor is the cursor whose contents are to be displayed in the list view. In Listing 4.16, there is as yet no cursor to display, so the actual parameter is `null`. The point of the rest of this chapter is to replace that value with the cursor full of data, acquired asynchronously from a database.

The first step as just described is to ask the LoaderManager to start a loader. That takes two lines of code, as shown in Listing 4.17.

Listing 4.17   **Initializing the Loader**

```java
public class LoaderActivity extends ListActivity {
    private static final int DATA_LOADER = -8954;

    // ...

    @Override
    protected void onCreate(Bundle state) {
        super.onCreate(state);

        SimpleCursorAdapter adapter = new SimpleCursorAdapter(
            this,
            R.layout.list_row,
            null,
            FROM,
            TO,
            0);

        setListAdapter(adapter);

        Bundle args = getIntent().getExtras();
        getLoaderManager().initLoader(DATA_LOADER, args, this);
    }

    // ...

}
```

The first argument to the call to initLoader is the name of the loader to be initialized. It is an integer: any integer unique across the application will do.

Recall that the onCreate method for this Activity will be called many times, sometimes more than once in a second. Creating a new loader instance each time onCreate is called would be wasteful. Instead, when initLoader is called it checks to see if a loader with the given name already exists. Only if none exists does it initialize and start a new one.

The second argument is the parameters passed to loader creation. They will reappear in a moment.

The third argument to initLoader is the callback handler. In a fractal-like repetition of the way that the Android framework calls an Activity with lifecycle events, the LoaderManager will call the callback handler with events representing the lifecycle of the Loader.

Expressing interactions between a process and an asynchronous collaborator as a stream of events is a pattern that will become an important architectural tool throughout the rest of this book. In this case, there are three events: onCreateLoader, onLoadFinished, and onLoaderReset.

To receive these events, the callback handler must implement the interface
LoaderManager.LoaderCallbacks<T> (which declares those three methods), where T is the
type of the object the loader will return. In this case, that object will be a Cursor. Listing 4.18
illustrates extending the LoaderActivity to accept loader lifecycle events.

Listing 4.18 **Accepting Loader Events**

```
public class LoaderActivity
    extends ListActivity
    implements LoaderManager.LoaderCallbacks<Cursor>
{

    private static final int DATA_LOADER = -8954;

    @Override
    public Loader<Cursor> onCreateLoader(int id, Bundle args) { }

    @Override
    public void onLoadFinished(Loader<Cursor> l, Cursor c) { }

    @Override
    public void onLoaderReset(Loader<Cursor> c) { }

    @Override
    protected void onCreate(Bundle state) {
        super.onCreate(state);

        SimpleCursorAdapter adapter = new SimpleCursorAdapter(
            this,
            R.layout.list_row,
            null,
            FROM,
            TO,
            0);

        setListAdapter(adapter);

        Bundle args = getIntent().getExtras();
        getLoaderManager().initLoader(DATA_LOADER, args, this);
    }

    // ...

}
```

At some point after the call to initLoader, the LoaderManager will call the callback handler—in
this case, the Activity—to request a Loader. This is the first of the three lifecycle events. Because the
goal here is to load a cursor, this Activity will supply a CursorLoader, as shown in Listing 4.19.

Listing 4.19 **Creating a Cursor Loader**

```java
public class LoaderActivity
    extends ListActivity
    implements LoaderManager.LoaderCallbacks<Cursor>
{
    private static final int DATA_LOADER = -8954;

    @Override
    public Loader<Cursor> onCreateLoader(int id, Bundle args) {
        return new CursorLoader(
            this,
            DataProvider.URI,
            new String[] {
                DataProvider.Columns.ID,
                DataProvider.Columns.FNAME,
                DataProvider.Columns.LNAME},
            DataProvider.Columns.LNAME + "=?",
            new String[] { args.getString(DataProvider.Columns.LNAME) },
            DataProvider.Columns.LNAME + " DESC");
    }

    @Override
    public void onLoadFinished(Loader<Cursor> l, Cursor c) { }

    @Override
    public void onLoaderReset(Loader<Cursor> c) { }

    @Override
    protected void onCreate(Bundle state) {
        super.onCreate(state);

        SimpleCursorAdapter adapter = new SimpleCursorAdapter(
            this,
            R.layout.list_row,
            null,
            FROM,
            TO,
            0);

        setListAdapter(adapter);

        Bundle args = getIntent().getExtras();
        getLoaderManager().initLoader(DATA_LOADER, args, this);
    }

    // ...

}
```

There are two things to notice in the new code. The first is that the bundle that was passed into the LoaderManager at initialization as the second argument, appears here as the parameter args. The code uses a value in that bundle as the argument to the query WHERE clause.

More important, though, is that the constructor parameters to the CursorLoader are almost identical to the parameters to a database query statement: URI, projection, restriction, restriction args, and ordering. The returned instance of the CursorLoader contains a complete, encapsulated representation of the query to be run.

Once the loader manager has the Loader, it runs it asynchronously. As mentioned earlier, CursorLoader inherits from AsyncTaskLoader, which uses a new instance of an AsyncTask to run the query embodied in the loader in the background. Figure 4.4 illustrates the entire lifecycle.

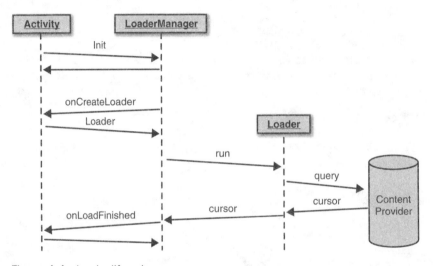

Figure 4.4   Loader lifecycle

The Activity initialized the loader. The call returns immediately. At some later point, the loader manager calls back to the Activity to obtain a Loader. The Loader creates a new instance of a subclass of AsyncTask and runs it, passing the query parameters.

Running on a background thread, the AsyncTask queries the database and eventually obtains a cursor full of data. In its onPostExecute method, it calls back to a completion method in the Loader, which in turn calls back to the Activity's onLoadFinished method, to deliver the cursor. This is the second loader lifecycle event.

Listing 4.20 shows the completely implemented activity.

Listing 4.20   **Complete Cursor Loader**

```
public class LoaderActivity
    extends ListActivity
    implements LoaderManager.LoaderCallbacks<Cursor>
{

    private static final int DATA_LOADER = -8954;

    @Override
    public Loader<Cursor> onCreateLoader(int id, Bundle args) {
        return new CursorLoader(
            this,
            DataProvider.URI,
            new String[] {
                DataProvider.Columns.ID,
                DataProvider.Columns.FNAME,
                DataProvider.Columns.LNAME},
            DataProvider.Columns.LNAME + "=?",
            new String[] { args.getString(DataProvider.Columns.LNAME) },
            DataProvider.Columns.LNAME + " DESC");
    }

    @Override
    public void onLoadFinished(Loader<Cursor> l, Cursor c) {
        ((SimpleCursorAdapter) getListAdapter()).swapCursor(c);
    }

    @Override
    public void onLoaderReset(Loader<Cursor> c) {
        ((SimpleCursorAdapter) getListAdapter()).swapCursor(null);
    }

    @Override
    protected void onCreate(Bundle state) {
        super.onCreate(state);

        SimpleCursorAdapter adapter = new SimpleCursorAdapter(
            this,
            R.layout.list_row,
            null,
            FROM,
            TO,
            0);

        setListAdapter(adapter);
```

```
        Bundle args = getIntent().getExtras();
        getLoaderManager().initLoader(DATA_LOADER, args, this);
    }

    // ...

}
```

Upon receiving the cursor from the Loader, the `onLoadFinished` method simply swaps the new cursor into the adapter created earlier in `onCreate`. Suddenly the contents of the cursor appear in the list view.

There is one more thing to notice. The loader does conform to one of the two AsyncTask patterns previously described. It is cancellable.

Although it is not obvious from the code, the LoaderManager observes lifecycle events for the Activity to which a Loader is attached. When it determines that the related Activity is being destroyed and that no other instance of the same Activity will immediately replace it (that is, when this is not just a screen rotation or similar event), it properly cancels the Loader.

As noted earlier, it might not be possible to cancel a query in mid-process. The `CursorLoader` comes as close as possible. It attempts to cancel the query, and discards the result as quickly as possible should the cancel fail.

It also calls the registered callback handler to notify it that the Loader has been cancelled. This is the third loader lifecycle event, and it is handled by the code in Listing 4.20 by replacing the cursor in the view adapter with `null`.

The loader demonstrates smart use of an AsyncTask in several ways:

- The details of the task are well hidden from the client. Although getting to this point was a bit complicated, in the end the code looks very much like our original ideal. There is an object that embodies the query and a method call when the query completes. The mechanism by which the query is run in the background is nearly invisible.

- The task is, as much as possible, cancellable. When the requested cursor is no longer useful, it is discarded as quickly as possible. It does not pin memory or busy the CPU for data that it already knows it does not need.

- The LoaderManager makes smart use of the lifecycle of an AsyncTask. If the loader for a particular dataset might be useful to some future Activity, the manager can let it run to completion, even though the Activity that requested the data is long gone. Instead, the manager delivers the loaded data to a new instance of the Activity when it becomes available.

AsyncTasks: What Went Wrong

It is easy to understand how developers end up using AsyncTasks incorrectly. When an aspiring Java developer creates her first Java application in an IDE, she probably sees skeleton code provided by the IDE, that looks something like Listing 4.21.

Listing 4.21 **A Skeleton Java Application**

```
public class AwesomeNewApp {

    public static void main(String... args) {
        // ...
    }
}
```

If this same programmer decides to take up Android development, the exact same IDE will generate code like that in Listing 4.22 for her first attempt at an Android app.

Listing 4.22 **A Skeleton Android Application**

```
public class AwesomeNewApp extends Activity {

    protected void onCreate(Bundle state) {
        // ...
    }
}
```

"Ah ha!" she says, and in her mind forms the model shown in Table 4.1.

Table 4.1 **A Naïve Model**

Role	Desktop App	Android App
Application File	.jar	.apk
Application Class	myClass	myActivity
Initialization Method	public static void main	protected void onCreate

Building on this model, the developer crams more and more functionality into an Activity. Of course, an experienced developer will factor some behavior into new packages and classes, to keep things modular. Nonetheless, a beginning Android programmer is likely to build an application in which one or more Activites are the center of the design.

To build great Android applications, it helps a lot to understand that they are, as pointed out in Chapter 3, web applications. A developer with Table 4.2 in mind will build programs that are more stable, behave more consistently, and are more delightful.

Table 4.2 **The Android Model**

Role	Web App	Android App
Application File	.war	.apk
View/Controller	servlet	activity
Business tier	manager/session bean	service
Persistence tier	DAL/model	Provider

In this more accurate model, AsyncTasks make sense: They are a way to get small, slow tasks out of the way, so that the UI can be responsive and blindingly fast.

Updating the model, synchronizing with remote data, and business computations belong elsewhere. They belong in Services, described in Chapter 6, "Processes and Bound Services."

Summary

This chapter has been a deep dive into the architecture of the AsyncTask. AsyncTask is a modest tool for moving the execution of small bits of code off the main thread and onto a worker thread. The exploration revealed the following points:

- AsyncTasks are type-safe templates and must be subclassed to be used. To execute a task, one creates a new instance of the subclass and calls its `execute` method. An instance can be executed only once.

- The template method of an AsyncTask, `doInBackground` is run on an Executor's worker thread. The default Executor, the `SERIAL_EXECUTOR`, executes tasks one at a time in order, but not necessarily on a single thread. It is possible to use other Executors.

- It is not possible to execute code on a background thread simply by wrapping it in an AsyncTask. Because code moved into an AsyncTask is executed on another thread, many normal Java keywords—`break`, `continue`, `throw`, and `return`—have an entirely different meaning from what they had in their original position. More important, though, the basic block structure of the Java language practically guarantees that such tasks will contain concurrency errors.

- AsyncTasks have lifecycles that are quite different from those of the Android components with which they interact. The incongruence of the two kinds of lifecycle can lead to memory leaks and application failure.

- AsyncTasks can be quite effective for the purposes for which they were originally conceived: small autonomous or cancellable tasks. Android Loaders, `CursorLoaders` in particular, are examples of the effective use of AsyncTasks.

AsyncTasks have been put to many uses for which they were never intended and for which they are frequently inappropriate. Most of the time this misuse stems from a misunderstanding of Android's architecture on the part of the developer. Understanding Android applications as Web-apps makes it obvious that AsyncTasks make sense for small, local tasks, but not for heavy lifting.

Looper/Handler

The ants go marching one by one. Hurrah! Hurrah!

Children's song

Although AsyncTasks are the first concurrency construct that most developers encounter when they start working with Android, they are not its central concurrency construct. The basic concurrency construct in Android is the Looper/Handler.

Introducing the Looper/Handler

The Looper/Handler framework, like several other important parts of Android's internal architecture, was probably inspired by the BeOS operating system—in particular, its `BLooper` and `BHandler` classes.

The Looper framework is an extension of the safe publication idiom, introduced Chapter 2, "Java Concurrency," and shown again in Figure 5.1. The idiom consists of a drop box and a lock on that drop box.

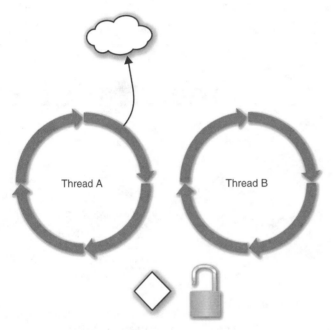

Figure 5.1   Safe publication

The essential point of the idiom is that an object that is not itself thread-safe can be published safely from one thread into another, by passing it through a correctly synchronized intermediate. The transfer is safe, as long as the sender retains no references to the passed object—and, of course, the passed object retains no references to objects owned by the source thread.

For simplicity, the example in Chapter 2 used a single-item drop box to hold the passed object while in transit. The Android Looper is an extension of the safe publication idiom that uses a sorted queue for object publication, instead of the simple drop box.

The Looper framework is illustrated in Figure 5.2. The Worker Thread is the thread into which the object will be published. The MessageQueue takes the place of the drop box. Clients seize the lock on the MessageQueue and enqueue an object to be passed. The Worker Thread seizes the same lock and dequeues the object. The only difference from the Chapter 2 idiom is that instead of holding a single item, the MessageQueue holds many, and establishes the order in which they are published.

The Handler is an added feature in the Looper/Handler framework. It abstracts away some the details of the underlying thread and MessageQueue.

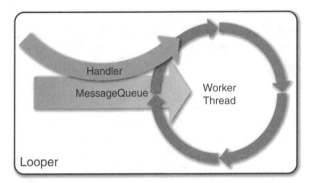

Figure 5.2   The Looper framework

The Looper framework consists of four Java classes and some native C code. The Java classes are as follows:

- `android.os.Looper`
- `android.os.Handler`
- `android.os.MessageQueue`
- `android.os.Message`

There is one additional helper class:

- `android.os.HandlerThread`

Basic Looper/Handler

The Looper is more than a simple publication mechanism. Its goal is to transfer a small amount of work, a task, from a source thread to the Looper's worker thread, for execution. It is simply an event queue powered by a single Java worker thread. When initialized with a Looper, a thread acquires two special features:

- A reference to a single instance of `MessageQueue`.
- The queue manager, the Looper's `loop` method, that is called from the worker thread's `run` method.

When a Java thread is initialized as a `Looper`, its `run` method calls `Looper.loop`. The `loop` method is a nonterminating loop that removes tasks from the Looper's `MessageQueue` and calls back to the Handler that enqueued them, from the Looper's worker thread, to get them processed.

Walking through the execution of a single task will illustrate the process. Suppose that some thread—called the source thread here—has a task that it would like to have executed by another thread, the worker thread, which has been initialized with a Looper. Figure 5.3 demonstrates.

The source thread begins (Figure 5.3, pane 1) by creating a new Handler for the target Looper:

```
Handler handler = new Handler(looper);
```

The variable looper is a reference to the worker thread's Looper. After the assignment, the variable handler contains a reference to a Handler object, which, in turn, holds a reference to the worker thread's MessageQueue.

A single Handler can be used to enqueue many tasks. Once the code running on the source thread has a reference to a Handler, it can use that Handler to create, enqueue, and process as many tasks as it likes.

Once the source thread has a reference to a Handler for the target worker thread, it uses that Handler to obtain a Message object from a pool. It attaches the task that it would like executed on the worker thread to the Message and then uses the Handler to enqueue the Message for the Looper (see Figure 5.3, pane 2):

```
Message msg = handler.obtainMessage(DELIVER_STUFF, stuff);
handler.sendMessage(msg);
```

The Handler uses correct synchronization to enqueue the Message, with its reference to the task, on the Looper's MessageQueue (Figure 5.3, pane 3). Of course, all the rules from the preceding chapters apply. If the passed task object is not itself thread-safe, the source thread must delete all references to it and to anything to which it refers. Similarly, the task must not hold any back references to objects in use by the source thread.

All the code, thus far, has run on the source thread. Once the Message is enqueued on the Looper's MessageQueue, though, its ownership is transferred to the Looper's worker thread. Eventually the Message is dequeued from the MessageQueue in the Looper's loop method on the Looper's worker thread. The Looper hands the dequeued message back to the Handler that originally enqueued it—still on the worker thread—for processing (Figure 5.3, pane 4). The Handler is responsible for processing the Message and its associated task in a callback method on the worker thread.

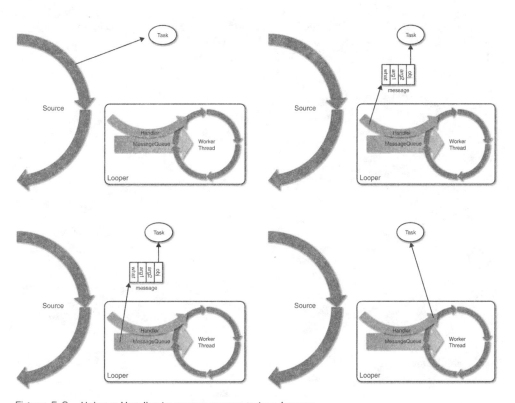

Figure 5.3   Using a Handler to pass a message to a Looper

Delegating Execution

The Looper/Handler framework provides two idioms for task processing. Although a single underlying mechanism supports both idioms, they are completely distinct. When trying to understand the framework, it helps to think of them as entirely different tools that, because of environmental constraints, have been crammed into a single implementation.

Posting a Runnable

The simplest way of delegating execution to another thread using the Looper/Handler framework is a collection of methods on Handler whose names begin with post .... These methods take as an argument a Runnable, which becomes the payload that is transferred to the worker thread. When one of the Handler post ... methods is invoked, the Handler, internally, obtains a Message object, attaches the Runnable to it, and enqueues the Message on the MessageQueue for the Looper with which the Handler is associated.

As illustrated in Figure 5.3, when a Message is removed from the MessageQueue by the target Looper, it is passed back to the Handler that originally enqueued it, for processing.

The `Handler` internally recognizes the `Message`'s attached `Runnable`, extracts it, and calls its `run` method. Listing 5.1 demonstrates posting a `Runnable` that starts an animation after a short delay.

Listing 5.1   **Naïve Delayed Animation**

```
private uiHandler;

@Override
@SuppressLint("HandlerLeak")
public void onCreate(Bundle state) {
    super.onCreate(state);

    // ...

    uiHandler = new Handler();
}

// ...

private void revealButtonDelayed() {
    uiHandler.postDelayed(
        new Runnable() {
            @Override
            public void run() {
                button.setVisibility(View.VISIBLE);
                ViewAnimationUtils
                    .createCircularReveal(button, ctr, ctr, 0, buttonDiameter)
                    .start();
            } },
        BUTTON_DELAY);
}
```

When a Handler is created without explicitly specifying a target Looper as an argument to the Handler's constructor, the Handler, by default, uses the Looper for the thread on which the constructor is run. If the current thread has not been initialized as a Looper, attempting to create a Handler without explicitly specifying a target Looper will cause a runtime exception.

In Listing 5.1, the Handler to which the variable `uiHandler` refers targets the Looper associated with the main thread. This is guaranteed because the `onCreate` method always runs on the main thread. It works because Android's main thread, it turns out, is the worker thread for a Looper. The static method `Looper.getMainLooper` is another way to get the same Looper, the Looper for the main thread, and it can be used from nearly any environment.

The code in the listing submits a Runnable that will start an animation that reveals `button` after `BUTTON_DELAY` milliseconds. There is a serious flaw, and one that should by now be familiar, in the code in Listing 5.1. Consider what happens if the fragment is executed just before the user rotates her device.

All the concerns that applied to AsyncTasks apply here. The immediate source of failure will be an exception thrown by the animation framework when it attempts to animate a button that is no longer part of the active view hierarchy. Remember that when the device is rotated, the entire view hierarchy is discarded and replaced with a new one.

In addition, recall that because the `Runnable` in Listing 5.1 is an anonymous class, it holds a reference to the surrounding Activity. The Activity cannot be garbage collected until the `Runnable` is freed, `BUTTON_DELAY` milliseconds hence.

These problems can be addressed in a number of ways. Choosing among them requires a clear understanding of the specifics. One could naively apply a broad, generic concurrency pattern. In this particular case, however, there is a much more lightweight solution. It is illustrated in Listing 5.2.

Listing 5.2 **Improved Delayed Animation**

```
Runnable animator;
private uiHandler;

@Override
@SuppressLint("HandlerLeak")
public void onCreate(Bundle state) {
    super.onCreate(state);

    // ...

    handler = new Handler();
}

@Override
public void onPause() {
    if (null != animator) {
        handler.removeCallbacks(animator);
        animator = null;
    }
    super.onPause();
}

// ...

private void showButton() {
    if (animator != null) { return; }
```

```
Runnable anim = new Runnable() {
    @Override
    public void run() {
        button.setVisibility(View.VISIBLE);
        ViewAnimationUtils
            .createCircularReveal(button, ctr, ctr, 0, buttonDiameter)
            .start();
        animator = null;
    }
};

uiHandler.postDelayed(anim, BUTTON_HIDE_DELAY);
animator = anim;
}
```

The important insight is that all the code in the example is running on a *single thread*, the main thread. There is no need for complex synchronization or locking. In addition, because a single thread executes all the code, each method is atomic with respect to the others. The thread that executes the `run` method of the animation Runnable must return from that method before it can execute any other method. In particular, this implies that the execution of the methods `run` and `onPause` are mutually exclusive.

Consider the possible states for Listing 5.2. In the initial state, the variable `animator` is null and a call to `onPause` will simply call `super.onPause`. A call to `showButton` in the initial state will execute the entire method, enqueueing the delayed animation and setting `animator` non-null. The only way that `animator` can be set non-null is when an animation is queued.

There are two ways of returning to the initial state. The first way is through the normal completion of the animator. The main thread dequeues the Message containing the animation Runnable and executes it, starting the animation. Once it does that, no animation task is still queued and `animator` is reset to null, the initial state. Figure 5.4 illustrates a typical execution of the two methods.

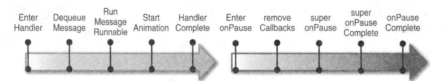

Figure 5.4   Typical execution

The second way of returning to the initial state is that `onPause` is called while an animation task is in the message queue. In this case, `animator` is not null so `onPause` removes the message to which it refers from the message queue, and sets `animator` to `null`—the initial state. The only way that `animator` can be set `null` is when a message is dequeued. In short, `animator` is non-null only during the time that an animation Runnable is in the queue.

Note also that when the Message is dequeued in `onPause`, there are no longer any dangling references to the Runnable. Because of that, the Runnable is eligible for garbage collection and will not prevent the Activity, to which it has an implicit pointer, from being garbage collected.

All the code in Listing 5.2 must run on the main thread because it manipulates view objects. Android view objects must never be touched from any other thread. Because they run on the same thread, the two methods—the Runnable's `run` and the Activity's `onPause`—are run asynchronously, but not concurrently.

It is interesting to consider how different the solution would have to be were this not the case—if `run` and `onPause` could run concurrently. At a minimum, the variable `animator` would have to be volatile because it would be accessed from more than one thread. More troublesome, though, is that if the Activity's `onPause` and the animation Runnable's `run` methods could run on different threads, they would not be atomic with respect to one another; there would be no happens-before relationship between them.

In such a scenario, there is an opportunity for a race in the interval between the time the Runnable is removed from the MessageQueue and the time its `run` method completes. The `onPause` method is supposed to cancel all animations. If it happens to execute during this interval it could not, without additional synchronization, guarantee that the `run` method hadn't scheduled a new animation, after it completed. Figure 5.5 illustrates this race condition: the worker thread dequeues a message and starts an animation, even after `onPause` completes.

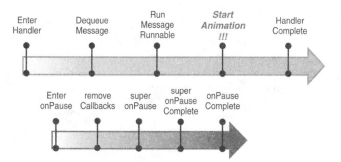

Figure 5.5   Race condition

This hypothetical situation—`onPause` and `run` executing on different threads—is only a little more difficult. It is definitely not insurmountable. Another handful of lines of code would fix it. The point, though, is that because `run` and `onPause` *must* run on the same thread, that handful of lines is the very best kind of code: code you don't need. The use of a Looper/Handler in Listing 5.2 does not imply massive synchronization and a profusion of concurrency constructs. Instead, after clear-eyed evaluation of the actual situation, it turns out that a very simple solution works just fine.

Enqueueing a Message

Although posting Runnables is very convenient, there are important problems with using them as a way of delegating execution.

The first problem is architectural. An application in which any component, anywhere, can post a Runnable to any Handler can quickly become a maintenance nightmare. Code enqueued to execute in some other place at some other time can be extremely hard to debug.

Also, because it is the central concurrency mechanism in Android, nearly every event of any kind that affects an application is represented, at some point in its lifecycle, as a Message enqueued for processing by a Looper. During some animations, for instance, there are events that occur every 17ms or so. Add to this all the events originating from the network, such as the keyboard, geo-location sensors, and whatever other source might show up. Together, they amount to hundreds of events every second.

That's a lot of events. If each event required creating a new Runnable object and then garbage collecting that object when it was no longer needed, the garbage collector would be very busy indeed. As a very sensible optimization, the Looper/Handler framework supports a pool of recyclable Message objects. Instead of transporting a Runnable, the Message object can itself identify a task to be performed and supply a few parameters for it.

There are several ways to get a Message from the pool. Probably the most convenient is to get it from the Handler that will enqueue and process it. A collection of overloaded methods on `Handler` named `obtainMessage...` retrieve and initialize the Message from the pool. For example:

```
Handler handler = new Handler(looper);
handler.obtainMessage(OP_SHOW_BUTTON).sendToTarget();
```

The call to `obtainMessage` returns a `Message` with its `what` field initialized to `OP_SHOW_BUTTON` (a Java `int`) and its `target` field—the field that contains a reference to the Handler to which the Message will be passed for processing—initialized with a reference to `handler`. The call to `sendToTarget` causes the Message to be handed back to `handler` to be enqueued on Looper's message queue.

> ### Note
>
> #### Method Overloading
>
> An *overloaded* method is one that has multiple signatures but a single name. For instance, the Handler methods `obtainMessage()`, `obtainMessage(int)`, `obtainMessage(int, int, int)`, `obtainMessage(int, int, int, Object)`, and `obtainMessage(int, Object)` are collectively an example of an overloaded method, `obtainMessage`.

When using this idiom, the behavior associated with a message is in the Handler that processes that message and not, as it was in the Runnable idiom, in the message itself. Listing 5.3 is an implementation of the feature originally implemented in Listing 5.2 using only Messages. This idiom and its `switch` statement are extremely common in Android code.

Listing 5.3   **Messaged Delayed Animation**

```java
private static final int OP_START_ANIMATION = -1;

private boolean animating;
private Handler handler;

@Override
@SuppressLint("HandlerLeak")
public void onCreate(Bundle state) {
    super.onCreate(state);

    // ...

    handler = new Handler() {
        @Override
        public void handleMessage(Message msg) {
            switch (msg.what) {
                case OP_START_ANIMATION:
                    animateButton();
                    break;
                default:
                    super.handleMessage(msg);
            }
        }
    };
}

@Override
public void onPause() {
    if (animating) {
        handler.removeMessages(OP_START_ANIMATION);
        animating = false;
    }
    super.onPause();
}

// ...

private void showButton() {
    if (animating) { return; }
    handler.sendMessageDelayed(
        handler.obtainMessage(OP_START_ANIMATION),
        BUTTON_HIDE_DELAY);
    animating = true;
}
```

```
void animateButton() {
    button.setVisibility(View.VISIBLE);
    ViewAnimationUtils
        .createCircularReveal(button, ctr, ctr, 0, buttonDiameter)
        .start();
    animating = false;
}
```

The analysis of this implementation is nearly identical to that of the code in Listing 5.2. The only change is that, instead of passing an object that will actually be executed, showButton now enqueues only a recyclable Message, containing an opcode in its what field. The case statement in the Handler switches on opcode values to call the appropriate method: code that would, in the Runnable idiom, have been the contents of the Runnable's run method. After handleMessage completes, the Handler automatically returns the Message to the message pool.

Although the recyclable message idiom is much more lightweight, it is also more limited. A Runnable can have nearly any conceivable behavior and, like a closure, can inherit state from the surrounding environment. A Message is only data. It can only invoke behaviors already in the Handler case statement and can only transfer data that is specifically attached to it. These limitations, however, can make code clearer and more thread-safe. Although the choice is up to the developer, the lightweight idiom is preferable in all except the simplest cases.

It is important to reiterate that the Handler used in all three of the preceding examples has the potential to cause memory leaks. Because it is an inner class, it has an implicit pointer to the Activity that contains it. Messages enqueued using the Handler hold a pointer to that Handler. Once a message is enqueued, the MessageQueue, in turn, holds a reference to the Message. The MessageQueue is a very long-lived object referred to by the thread that powers the Looper. Until the last message from a given Handler has been removed from the queue, neither the Handler nor the Activity to which it refers is eligible for garbage collection.

In the examples in this chapter, this is not significant because onPause removes all the Messages that refer to the Handler from the queue before the Activity is eligible for destruction. If the next developer who modifies this code is not as careful, though, it would be all too easy to leak the Activity. To prevent this possibility, Android Lint recommends that all Handlers be static inner class and hold at most a WeakReference to their Activity.

This is the heart of the Looper/Handler framework: a single thread servicing a single queue on which any number of other threads can enqueue Messages using Handlers. The Handler gives very fine-grained control over how the messages are processed, being both the producer that is invoked on the local thread to enqueue Messages for eventual processing, and the consumer that runs on a Looper's worker thread and processes those Messages.

Some Gory Details

The previous sections provide most of the information necessary to use the Looper/Handler framework. There are some details, however, that can help you to use it more effectively.

Handlers and Messages

A Message is a small, simple object: nearly a POJO (Plain Old Java Object). Most of its fields are actually managed by the Handler.

Messages themselves are not thread-safe. None of the Message object's fields are final or volatile. An enqueueing thread must not retain a reference to a Message that has been enqueued for a different thread.

Figure 5.6 is a schematic diagram of a Message.

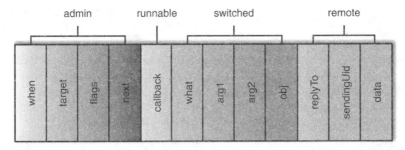

Figure 5.6   The Message

As the figure indicates, there are four groups of fields with related purposes:

- Admin group: used by the framework for internal management
- Runnable: Runnable execution
- Switched: Switched execution
- Remote: Inter-process communication

The Admin Fields

The framework uses the administrative fields for basic message processing. All the fields are private to the framework (package-protected). Of most interest are when, the time at which the message is to be processed, and target, mentioned previously, the reference to the Handler to which the message will be given for processing.

The when field implements a timed queue. As demonstrated in the previous examples, messages can be enqueued for execution at specific future times. The Looper/Handler message queue is sorted by the when field and the Looper will not dequeue and process a message until the current time, as measured by SystemClock.uptimeMillis, is greater than or equal to the time stored in the Message's when field. Several overloaded Handler methods support timed delays:

- postAtTime(runnable, ..., uptimeMillis)
- postDelayed(runnable, delayMillis)
- sendMessageAtTime(message, uptimeMillis)
- sendMessageDelay(message, delayMillis)

Although the unadorned post... and send... methods simply set when to be the current time, these methods enable clients of the framework to submit messages for execution either at specific times or at some delta from the current time. When using the absolute time version of these post methods, be sure to use SystemClock.uptimeMillis and not System.currentTimeMillis!

The target field is a reference to the Handler to which a message will be given for processing. There are several ways to set the target. Interestingly, all but one of them are irrelevant.

Calling one of Handler's overloaded obtain... methods returns a Message whose target field is preset to refer to the called Handler. Similarly, all the static obtain... methods on Message take a Handler as the first argument. In fact, the Handler methods simply call the Message methods, passing this as their first argument. There is even a third possibility, a setTarget method on Message instances.

None of these ways of setting the Message target is significant in any way. When a Message is enqueued for processing, the Handler that enqueues it sets its target, as part of the enqueueing process, to refer to itself. The Handler that enqueues the Message is always its target. Listing 5.4 is an example of code that is seriously confusing but enqueues a Message with what set to OP_CONFUSION, on looper1's MessageQueue, for processing by handler1.

Listing 5.4 **Target Confusion**

```
Handler handler1 = new Handler(looper1);
Handler handler2 = new Handler(looper2);

handler1.sendMessage(handler2.obtainMessage(OP_CONFUSION));
```

Although the Message is obtained from handler2, enqueueing it with handler1 sets the target to be handler1.

> **Note**
>
> `Message.setTarget()`? **Srsly!?**
>
> One wonders about the wisdom of exposing this method. The possibilities for misuse completely dwarf any possibility for benefit—if there even is one!
>
> **Consider:**
>
> `Message msg = Message.obtain();`
>
> `handler.sendMessage();`
>
> `msg.setTarget(null); //!!!`

The remaining admin field, `flag`, is used primarily for the `FLAG_IN_USE` bit. This bit is used to track the lifecycle of a `Message`. It is set when a Message is released into the message pool, cleared when it is removed from the pool, and checked when it is enqueued or released to the pool. If it is set at either of the two checks, an exception is thrown. This guarantees that Messages are never doubly freed back into the pool, and that they are never enqueued once they've been released. Despite its name, the bit is set only when the Message is in the pool and not in use. The other flag, `FLAG_ASYNCHRONOUS` affects scheduling and will be discussed shortly.

The Messaging Fields

The two non-overlapping sets of fields classified here as "Runnable" and "Switched" represent the two separate means of processing a `Message`, explored in the examples in Listings 5.2 and 5.3. If `callback` is non-null, the Handler completely ignores Switched fields and invokes the `run` method of the `Runnable` to which `callback` refers. This behavior can be changed. It is implemented in the `Handler` method `dispatchMessage`, which is not final and can be overridden.

If `callback` is null, `dispatchMessage` interprets the message as Switched. Switched messages are processed in one of two ways. If the Handler instance was initialized with an instance of `Handler.Callback`, that Callback's `handleMessage` method is called, passing the message. If the Handler instance does not have a `Handler.Callback`, or if the call to `Handler.Callback.handleMessage` returns `false` the Handler's own `handleMessage` method is called with the message. `Handler`, the base class, does implement `handleMessage`, but its implementation is empty: It will simply ignore all messages. A subclass of Handler that does not either pass a `Handler.Callback` or override `handleMessages` is useful only for posting Runnables.

Switched messages are typically processed with a `switch` on the Message `what` field. The Android source itself, AOSP, is full of this kind of use of the Looper/Handler framework.

The fields `arg1` and `arg2` are simple, `int` values, available for use as arguments to the code selected for execution by the `what` field. The third argument, `obj`, is a reference to an `Object` and thus enables the inclusion of arbitrary additional parameters. It also implies all the usual thread-safety constraints.

The Remote Fields

The remaining fields in the Message are used for inter-process communication. They will be discussed in Chapter 6, "Services, Processes, and IPC."

Starting a Looper

A Looper is, as mentioned at the beginning of this chapter, simply a queue manager, initialized with a single Java thread and a MessageQueue. Whereas there can be multiple Handlers associated with a single Looper, there can be only a single Looper associated with a given thread. Unlike Java's Executor framework, the Looper framework supports only a single thread servicing a single queue.

Initializing a thread as a Looper is a four-step process:

1. Create and start the thread.

2. From the running thread, call the static method `Looper.prepare`.

3. Perform any additional initialization.

4. From the running thread, call the static method `Looper.loop`. This method will not return until the Looper is stopped.

Listing 5.5 demonstrates a simple Looper.

Listing 5.5 **Looper Creation**

```
Thread looperThread = new Thread() {
    @Override
    public void run() {
        Looper.prepare();
        Looper.loop();
    }
};
looperThread.start();
```

Although `looperThread` is now running as a Looper, it is not very useful. The Looper/Handler framework does not provide any way to find the Looper that is associated with an arbitrary thread if one exists. Because there is no way to find the Looper associated with `looperThread`—even though there is one—there is no way to associate a Handler with it and therefore no way to submit or process work using it.

The Android documentation suggests creating a Handler as part of the initialization of the Looper thread, as shown in Listing 5.6.

Listing 5.6 **Looper Creation**

```
public volatile Handler mainHandler;

// ...

    Thread looperThread = new Thread() {
        @Override
        public void run() {
            Looper.prepare();
            mainHandler = new Handler();
            Looper.loop();
        }
    };
    looperThread.start();
```

There is a variant of the idiom shown in Listing 5.6. In this alternative, the publication of the reference to the Handler into the variable `mainHandler` is replaced by the publication of a reference to the Looper, using the method `Looper.myLooper`. The `myLooper` method returns the Looper with which the current thread has been initialized, and can be used at any time after the call to `Looper.prepare`.

Although the two variants are nearly equivalent, the code in Listing 5.6 might be clearer than the alternative when the Looper has a single specific purpose. A canonical Handler instantiated just before entering the loop can explicitly implement that purpose, thus simply and clearly expressing the function of the code.

Publishing a reference to a single Handler is sufficient, even if it will be necessary to add additional Handlers later. A call to the Handler method `getLooper` returns a reference to a Handler's Looper, for use in initializing other Handlers.

The code in Listing 5.6 contains a significant data race. As written, there is no simple way to tell when the assignment to `mainHandler` takes place. The `Thread` method `start` schedules the new thread and returns immediately. It makes no guarantees about when the newly scheduled thread will actually begin execution. The assignment to `mainHandler` might be visible as soon as `start` returns or only after the execution of hundreds of statements.

The Android convenience class `HandlerThread` avoids this race and makes creating a new Looper a completely straightforward process. Listing 5.7 demonstrates this.

Listing 5.7 **Looper Creation**

```
HandlerThread looperThread = new HandlerThread("AlternateLooper");
looperThread.start();
Looper looper = looperThread.getLooper(); // may block!
```

The `HandlerThread` internally looks a lot like Listing 5.6. It adds an additional synchronization mechanism in the `getLooper` method that blocks until the `HandlerThread` begins execution and initializes its Looper. When the method returns, eventually, `looper` is guaranteed to be non-null. Obviously, because it blocks, `HandlerThread.getLooper` should be called from code that is not extremely time-sensitive—perhaps at component initialization.

> **Note**
>
> Don't forget to `start` your threads!
>
> The code in Listing 5.7 will block permanently, unless there is a call to `looperThread`'s `start` method! Simply creating the thread does not schedule it for execution.

The Native Looper

Every Looper has a native shadow that is a near a mirror image of the Java framework but is written in C/C++. The native shadow has a native analog for each Looper/Handler framework Java component: `Message`, `MessageQueue`, `Handler` and the `Looper`. Perhaps surprisingly, the native Looper is scheduled on the same thread as the Java Looper. A Looper's worker thread, therefore, actually services *two* separate queues: the Java queue and the native queue. The native queue is polled before the Java queue.

It is the native Looper that surrenders the CPU when there are no messages ready for execution. When there are no schedulable messages in either queue, the native Looper yields the processor using the Linux **epoll** mechanism. `epoll` is a kernel primitive that enables a thread to wait for new data to appear in any of a set of file descriptors. Because it yields the processor in this way, a Looper can be awakened asynchronously by another thread that writes data to one of the file descriptors on which the Looper is waiting.

The `epoll` mechanism also supports timed-wait. This mechanism enables a thread to wait until either new data arrives or a specified amount of time elapses, whichever happens first. A Looper uses the `epoll` timed-wait mechanism to go to sleep, scheduling itself to be restarted at the time at which the next Message in its MessageQueue is scheduled for processing.

This is safe, even if the wake-up time is a considerable distance in the future. If a Message is enqueued by some other thread and must be scheduled before the sleeping Looper thread is scheduled to wake up, writing a byte to a canonical pipe (not surprisingly, called the `mWakeWritePipeFd`) will wake it up.

Nearly the only way to enqueue tasks on a Looper's native queue is to use the native framework. Because of this, most Loopers, with the obvious exception of main thread, never had any significant work in their native queue. Polling the native queue is only minor overhead.

As of Android 6.0, Marshmallow, the Looper/Handler framework exposes several new methods in Java. Among these is `MessageQueue.isIdle`, a method that queries the queue for scheduled tasks. It can be used to determine directly whether a Looper is idle or not.

There are also two new methods that provide direct Java access to the `epoll` mechanism: `MessageQueue.addOnFileDescriptorEventListener` and `MessageQueue.removeOnFile DescriptorEventListener`. These two methods enable Java code to register new file descriptors and callbacks, in the native Looper's `epoll` file descriptor wait set.

Scheduling and the Sync-Barrier

A discussion of details would not be complete without some consideration of the specifics of task scheduling. Task scheduling is implemented in the MessageQueue method `next`.

Perhaps the first thing to notice is that, because the MessageQueue's queue is a simple linked list sorted by execution time, the computational complexity of enqueueing a task is O(n). Because n is normally very small, the overhead is probably negligible in most cases. The normal case of scheduling a task without specifying the time at which it is to run, however, almost certainly will cause a scan of the entire queue. On a heavily used Looper, like that associated with the main thread, this overhead can be significant.

As described earlier, a Looper yields the processor by invoking native code. Just before the queue-polling code on the Java side of the framework passes control to the native half with the intention of yielding the CPU, it invokes any registered `MessageQueue.IdleHandlers`. This provides a mechanism through which code can release resources that are needed only while tasks are being processed. A network interface, for instance, might open a network connection as part of processing the first request delivered from the queue. It might then register a `MessageQueue.IdleHandler` to close that connection after the last request is completed.

The most interesting twist to task scheduling, however, is something called a **sync-barrier**. Sync-barriers appeared in Android in the JellyBean release. Sync-barriers are used to stall a Looper so that a concurrent task can be executed synchronously. In particular, Android 5.0, Lollypop, API level 21 and Material Design introduced a new UI architecture, optimized for animation and high-performance graphics. Among other changes, this architecture makes heavy use of a new, dedicated rendering thread separate from the main thread. The framework needs a way to suspend the execution of UI-related main thread tasks, while the render thread traverses the view tree to render the view.

Sync-barriers introduce a new dimension for tasks. In addition to the `post.../send...` distinction—Message/Runnable processing—since JellyBean, messages are also either synchronous or asynchronous. Asynchronous messages are simply messages that can be processed despite a sync-barrier. Android API level 22 provides the method `Message.setAsynchronous` that gives developers the capability to control this attribute of a task.

A sync-barrier is implemented as a Message with a null target. There is no way to create such a message, correctly, with the visible interface. It is possible only with the method `MessageQueue.postSyncBarrier`. As of Android version 6.0, this method is hidden with `@hide` and called only from code that traverses the view hierarchy. The synchronous/asynchronous distinction is relevant only on the main thread.

When the MessageQueue task scheduling code encounters a target-less message, it continues to scan the task queue but ignores any messages that have not been marked as asynchronous (their `FLAG_ASYNCHRONOUS` flag is set). If there are asynchronous messages ready for execution, they are scheduled normally. If no asynchronous message is ready for execution, the Looper yields the processor and schedules wake-up for the execution time of the first asynchronous task in the queue. If there are no asynchronous messages in the queue, the sleep time is −1, indefinite.

The only way to un-stall a blocked MessageQueue is to remove the sync-barrier explicitly. The hidden MessageQueue method `removeSyncBarrier` removes the barrier, wakes up the thread, and corrects the wake-up time to be the time of the next schedulable task.

The use of sync-barriers can have a surprising effect on the accuracy of scheduling on the main thread. Table 5.1 shows standard deviations for execution times for three different types of tasks. The test code used to create these measurements schedules trivial Messages for delivery at 10ms in the future and, upon execution, calculates the difference between the scheduled and actual execution times. The tests represented in the table were performed while running a simple, full-screen animation, and they were run on several different devices. Although specific standard deviation varied from device to device, the numbers shown in the table are characteristic.

A task scheduled on a freshly created Looper running only the test tasks had a standard deviation of less than .2 ms. The same test run on the main thread using a Message marked as asynchronous produced a slightly higher standard deviation. This is to be expected; the main thread, running an animation, is already busy.

The big effect comes when the task is run on the main thread and is not marked asynchronous. Under these circumstances, the standard deviation goes up by an order of magnitude, to a very significant 2 ms.

Table 5.1 **Execution Time Standard Deviation (Typical Device)**

Message Type	σ ms
Main thread, Synchronous	~2.00
Main thread, Asynchronous	~0.20
Worker	~0.17

Summary

The Looper is the basic concurrency structure in Android. It supports scheduled, asynchronous task execution in a safe and lightweight framework.

The Looper/Handler framework is quite complex. It has two halves, one Java and one native. The native half is based on the Linux `epoll` mechanism and supports waiting for a specified length of time, or for new data to be written into one of a set of file descriptors.

The framework supports the execution of several types of messages. It supports both the direct execution of a Java Runnable and a more frugal mode in which the code to be executed— usually in a `case` statement in the Handler method `handleMessage`—is selected using an opcode in the Message's `what` field.

The Android framework initializes the main thread, which is created as part of starting a new process for a new application with a Looper. The main thread is just the canonical Looper's worker thread, the thread on which UI components (and nearly everything else, except by special arrangement) are run. The main thread's Looper is always available via the `Looper` method `getMainLooper`.

A careful reader, after contemplating the Looper/Handler framework, could re-implement AsyncTasks in terms of Looper/Handlers. In fact, there is some evidence that this is exactly how the original AsyncTask was implemented. As noted previously, there are hints in the documentation—though none in readily accessible code—that AsyncTasks were, in the earliest versions of Android, run on a single thread. That thread was very likely a Looper.

Because Loopers are powered by a single thread, enqueueing a task that runs for thirty minutes will stall every other job in the queue for thirty minutes. The dreaded ANR, Application Not Responding error, results, exactly from stalling the main thread and preventing it from processing tasks in its MessageQueue in a timely way.

The semantics of the Looper/Handler framework—in-order execution on a single thread— are, as discussed in the preceding chapter, fairly appealing. They do mean, however, that a developer must be aware of the profiles of the tasks being enqueued. On the main thread, for instance, flipping the flag on a view object, computing the dimensions and location of a view object, and even painting the background of a large view object are all things that can be done reasonably. Network calls, database queries, and resizing an image are all things that cannot.

Services, Processes, and Binder IPC

Glendower: I can summon spirits from the vasty deep.

Hotspur: Why, so can I, or so can any man. But will they come when you do call for them?

Shakespeare, Henry IV

The Android Service component is a key resource for managing concurrent processes. Understanding it in some detail is essential to creating well-architected Android applications.

There are three reasons for using a Service in an application:

- **Architectural:** It makes sense, architecturally, to separate business logic from the UI that presents it. In general, anything that gets code out of Activity objects is a great idea.

- **Process priority:** Delegating a task to a Service can increase the priority of the process that hosts the Service. As discussed in Chapter 3, "The Android Application Model," the process that hosts the visible Activity has the highest priority. A Service, though, can also change the priority of its host process by declaring to the framework that it is performing useful work. A higher process priority decreases the probability that the task will be interrupted, even when the process is not hosting a visible Activity.

- **Inter-process communication (IPC):** A **bound Service**, described shortly, is the Android IPC tool.

The component called a Service is, actually, two different mechanisms, the **started service** and the **bound service**, wrapped up in a single package. Both mechanisms provide system-addressable components that can be used to execute tasks on other threads or even in other processes.

Service Basics

Whether started or bound, all Services are the same in some respects. One simple way of understanding them is as an Activity with no UI. That can sound a bit odd because an Activity's sole purpose is to power a UI. A review of the features common to all Services, however, will demonstrate that the comparison is apt.

Like any other Android component, a Service, whether bound or started, must subclass its component class (`Service` in this case). Also, like other components, a Service must be registered in its application's manifest as shown in Listing 6.1.

Listing 6.1 **Declaring a Service**

```
<manifest
  xmlns:android="http://schemas.android.com/apk/res/android"
  package="net.callmeike.android.exampleservice"
  >

  <application

    ...

    <service android:name=".ExampleService" />
  </application>

</manifest>
```

The Android framework reads an application's manifest when the application is installed. It registers the components it finds there, including Services, along with their attributes, in a system-wide lookup table. They stay in the table until the application is uninstalled.

The `exported` attribute in the Service's manifest declaration controls whether or not it is visible and can be used from other applications. By default, a Service is not exported and not visible externally. The Service in Listing 6.1, for instance, cannot be used by other applications. Either declaring the Service `exported="true"`, or including an `intent-filter` (described below) in its declaration would make it externally visible.

Also, like other components, there is only one instance of a given Service at any time. An instance of the Service is created in response to the first request for it. Once created, the single instance responds to all subsequent requests—start or bind—until all those requests have been satisfied and the Service is either stopped or the last client unbinds. The Service instance is then destroyed. Subsequent requests create and use a new instance.

Like an Activity, a Service has a lifecycle that is implemented with callbacks. Unlike an Activity—and because a Service does not manage a UI—its lifecycle is fairly simple. It has fewer lifecycle states and also fewer callbacks. The four methods `onCreate`, `onStartCommand`, `onBind` and `onDestroy` are the essentials.

Because the `Service` class packages two different mechanisms, its interface is complicated by interface pollution. It contains the lifecycle methods for both interfaces. Although it can be useful to both start and bind a Service—a **hybrid service**—most implementations will not.

Also like an Activity, Service methods are always executed on the main thread of the process in which they run. It is very important to understand that a long-running task in a Service will stall the UI of the application hosting it, just as surely as would the same task running in an Activity. A Service with expensive methods must make arrangements to run those methods on a background thread.

Finally, like an Activity, the lifecycle of a Service affects the priority of the process that powers it. When a Service announces to the Android framework that it is performing work on behalf of a client, the priority of the host process will be higher than it would be if the process contained no working components.

The specifics of Service priority, especially bound Service priority, are fairly complex. As shown in Chapter 3, Figure 3.2, a process that contains an active Service will have priority that is lower (`oom_adj` value is higher) than that of the process that contains a visible Activity, but higher than that of a process that contains only Activities that are not visible. That just makes sense; when a process contains a Service that is doing useful work, it is more important than process that isn't doing anything. It is not, however, as important as the process that the user is currently viewing.

Process priority is among the most important reasons for using Services. Unless a long-running task is implemented in a Service, the Android system has no way of knowing that the task is running. It can lower the host process' priority and even reap that process, before the task completes. Services are the best solution to this problem, which was described in detail in Chapter 4, "AsyncTasks and Loaders."

Although a process that contains a running Service is less likely to be interrupted, there are no guarantees. There is a possibility, somewhat smaller on modern devices with their comparatively large memories, that a Service, even one that has announced that it is doing useful work, will be interrupted. The longer a task runs, the more likely it is to be interrupted.

Started Service Essentials

In general terms, a started Service is usually more autonomous. To start a Service, a client creates a small package of parameters, an Intent, and then uses the Intent as the argument to the `Context` method, `startService`. A Service receives the Intent asynchronously as an argument to its `onStartCommand` method. It performs the task represented by the Intent, frequently without any further interaction with the client. Like a method with `void` return type, started Services frequently do not return an explicit result. Figure 6.1 illustrates an Activity starting a Service, to perform an asynchronous task.

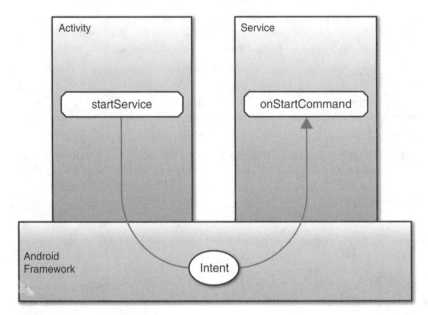

Figure 6.1   A started Service

> **Note**
>
> Figure 6.1 does not show process boundaries. When discussing Services, process boundaries are frequently irrelevant. As long as the Service on the right side of the figure is exported, the Activity on the left can send an Intent to it, whether it is in the same, or a different, process

As mentioned previously, the Android framework can be forced to interrupt a Service to make room for some other application. A started Service uses the value it returns from its onStartCommand method to request the way it would like the Android framework to handle such an interruption. There are, essentially, three possibilities.

The first possibility is that onStartCommand returns the flag START_NOT_STICKY. This flag indicates to the framework that it need not take any additional actions. If it must interrupt the started Service, the Service is marked as stopped and the framework makes no effort to restart it.

At the other extreme, the onStartCommand can return the flag START_REDELIVER_INTENT. This flag indicates to the framework that if it must stop the Service, it should restart it when conditions permit.

When the framework interrupts such a Service, it marks the Service as stopped. The framework restarts the Service, though, by redelivering the same Intent that started it in the first place. A Service can detect that it has been restarted by checking the second parameter to onStartCommand, the flags. If it is being restarted, the START_FLAG_REDELIVERY is set. Using START_REDELIVER_INTENT is a simple way of restarting idempotent tasks.

The last possibility is slightly more complicated. If onStartCommand returns the flag START_STICKY then the Service, when interrupted, is terminated but it is not marked as stopped. Instead, the framework will, when conditions permit, recreate and rerun the Service by calling its onStartCommand method again. It will not redeliver the original Intent, however. When restarted, the Intent parameter to the onStartCommand call will be null.

Bound Service Essentials

Figure 6.2 illustrates the second type of Service, the bound Service. At first glance, a bound Service appears to be an implementation of the Factory pattern.

To bind a Service, a client creates an Intent that is similar to one that might be used to start a Service. Instead of calling startService, though, it calls bindService. In addition to the Intent, it provides a reference to a callback handler, an implementation of the ServiceConnection interface.

The Service receives the Intent asynchronously, this time as the parameter to a call to its onBind method. In response to onBind it returns an instance of its managed object.

The Android framework, again asynchronously, invokes the onConnected method of the callback handler originally passed by the client. As a parameter to the call, it passes a reference to a managed object similar to the one returned from the onBind method. The client now has an instance of the Service-provided object and can interact with it in nearly the same way that it would any other Java object.

As a factory, a bound Service provides a level of abstraction between the type of the object returned to the client, and its actual implementation. In a second layer of abstraction, it is the Android framework that collects the result of the onBind call, and then passes that result—or something like it—in the call to onConnected. This will be important for one of the chief uses of a bound Service, inter-process communication, where the object's implementation can be in a different process.

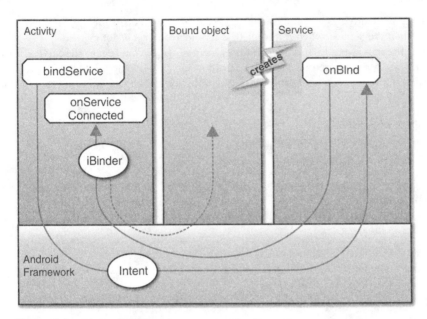

Figure 6.2   A bound Service

Intents

Both started and bound Services are selected by the Intent that is used to start them. The Intent must identify the Service that is the intended target of a call to `startService` or `bindService`. An Intent can do this in several ways. For an exhaustive description of Intents, their attributes, and their filters, refer to the Android documentation. Roughly, though, the mechanisms break down into two general categories: **explicit** and **implicit**.

An explicit Intent includes the name of a package (application) and the relative name of the specific class within that package that implements the Service. At best, an explicit Intent names exactly one Service in one specific application. At worst it names nothing at all.

Listing 6.2 demonstrates the construction of three identical explicit Intents (assuming the code is a fragment of an application named `net.callmeike.android.exampleservice`, that contains a Service named `net.callmeike.android.exampleservice.svc.ExampleService`).

Listing 6.2   **Explicit Intents**

```
Intent intent1 = new Intent(context, ExampleService.class);

Intent intent2 = new Intent();
intent2.setComponent(new ComponentName(
  context.getPackageName(),
```

```
    ExampleService.class.getName());

Intent intent3 = new Intent();
intent2.setComponent(new ComponentName(
  "net.callmeike.android.exampleservice",
  "net.callmeike.android.exampleservice.svc.ExampleService");
```

An important thing to notice here is that the explicit Intent is *not* retaining a reference either to the class object (ExampleService.class) or to the Context object passed to it. Although the simplest constructor in Listing 6.2, the one used to create intent1, takes both of these arguments, it uses them only to create name strings. As illustrated in the creation of intent3, it is entirely possible—though somewhat fragile—to create explicit Intents that name components in other applications, provided the names of those components are known.

An implicit Intent is an Intent that must be caught using an **intent filter**. An IntentFilter is an Android framework object that is used to match canonical Intent attributes: action, package, category, MIME type, and so on. IntentFilters for Services are created, as shown in Listing 6.3, as part of registering a Service, in its application's manifest.

When a Service registers an IntentFilter, it becomes a candidate to receive any Intent that matches the filter specifications (it is exported). In the example in Listing 6.3, the service ExampleService is registering to receive Intents whose action attribute is net.callmeike. android.exampleservice.PING.

Listing 6.3 **An IntentFilter**

```
<manifest
  xmlns:android="http://schemas.android.com/apk/res/android"
  package="net.callmeike.android.exampleservice"
  >

  <application>
    ...

    <service android:name=".ExampleService">
      <intent-filter>
        <action android:name="net.callmeike.android.exampleservice.PING" />
      </intent-filter>
    </service>
  </application>

</manifest>
```

As most Android users know, ambiguous Activity calls—a call to startActivity with an Intent that matches multiple Activites—are resolved by presenting the user with a system dialog and allowing her to choose among them. Think, for instance, of what happens when there are multiple browsers or multiple telephony apps installed on a device.

The disambiguation protocol for delivering in-flight Intents to a Service, on the other hand, is silent and, essentially, random. Because of this, it is wildly unsafe to use implicit Intents to launch Services. Although it has been unsafe since the origin of Android, it is only as of API 21, KitKat, that an Intent used in a call to `startService` must name a target application explicitly.

At the time of this writing, the Android documentation suggests that the Intent used to identify a Service must be an explicit Intent. Actually, that isn't necessary. It is sufficient that the Intent specify a unique target application, by specifying its package name. It is possible to do this minimally, using the Intent method `setPackage` with a `String` argument that is the fully qualified package name of the target application.

Obviously, this still leaves open the possibility of ambiguous Services. An ambiguous Service within an application, though, is just a bug, not a security problem.

Also important to understand, in the context of concurrency, is that the Intent that a client uses to invoke a Service is never the Intent that the Service receives as a result of being invoked. In particular, the code in Listing 6.4 always produces output that looks like this:

```
...
01-10 16:58:51.102 1953-1953/…servicesandbox I/SVC: intent == originalIntent: false
...
```

Listing 6.4 **Intent Identity**

```java
public class SimpleService extends Service {
  // ...

  private static Intent startIntent;

  @UiThread
  public static void start(Context ctxt) {
    if (null != startIntent) {
      throw new IllegalStateException("start called twice");
    }
    startIntent = new Intent(ctxt, SimpleService.class);
    ctxt.startService(startIntent);
  }

  // ...

  @UiThread
  @Override
  public int onStartCommand(Intent intent, int flags, int startId) {
    Log.i(TAG, "intent == originalIntent: " + (intent == startIntent));
    startIntent = null;
```

```
    startWork();
    return super.onStartCommand(intent, flags, startId);
  }

  // ...
}
```

There are two consequences to this. The first is that a Service need not be concerned about whether there are external references to the Intent that is passed to it. The Intent that the Service receives is a deep copy of the one the client used in its call to startService or bindService. The Intent to which the Service holds a reference is its own and the Service can use it without thread safety concerns.

The second consequence is that the Intent must be an object of which the Android system can make a deep copy. In Java the Cloneable interface is the canonical way of indicating that an object can be replicated. Android Intents are Cloneable but they actually support an even stronger contract, Parcelable. Objects that support the Parcelable contract can be transferred between Android processes.

Java's contract for objects that can be transferred between processes is the Serializable interface. A serializable object can be stored for reconstitution at some other place and time through a process called **marshaling**. The marshaled representation of the object can be **unmarshaled** in its new environment to create a new, different object that is effectively identical to the original.

The Parcelable interface, discussed in detail below, is Android's lightweight equivalent of Java Serializable. Clearly, an object that can be marshaled and unmarshaled can be copied. Because they are Parcelable, though, Intents can also be passed across process boundaries.

The Intent Service

The IntentService is probably the most common way of using a started Service. It is a simple, attractive, and elegant extension of the basic Service class that provides exactly the functionality that developers are actually looking for when they turn to AsyncTasks.

Recall from the previous section that unless the implementation of a Service specifically arranges an alternative, all its code is run on the UI thread. That makes it pretty useless as a way of implementing long-running tasks. Once again, the problem is getting tasks off the UI thread.

Chapter 3 discussed Android's naïve tool for concurrency, the AsyncTasks, and described the many problems with using them in an Activity context. It will be instructive, though, to reconsider them here, in the context of a Service.

Listing 6.5 shows a Service that executes tasks that are invoked with calls to onStartCommand, but on a background thread.

Listing 6.5   **The AsyncTask Service**

```
public class AsyncTaskService extends Service {
  private int running;

  // ...

  @UiThread
  public int onStartCommand(Intent intent) {
    running++;
    new AsyncTask<Intent, Void, Void>() {
      @UiThread protected void onPostExecute(Void result) { finishTask(); }
      @UiThread protected void onCancelled(Void result) { finishTask(); }
      @WorkerThread protected Void doInBackground(Intent... intent) {
        executeTask(intent[0]);
        return null;
      }
    }.execute(intent);
    return Service.START_NOT_STICKY;
  }

  @UiThread
  void finishTask() {
    if (0 >= --running) { stopSelf(); }
  }

  @WorkerThread
  void executeTask(Intent intent) {
    // do task work...
  }
}
```

First of all, note that there is nothing constraining AsyncTasks to use solely in Activities. They work perfectly well in other components.

The AsyncTask in Listing 6.5 is simply a portal to a background thread. When a client calls the startService method, the parameter Intent is passed to the Service in the call to onStartCommand. The implementation of onStartCommand, in the AsyncTaskService immediate forwards that Intent to a new, anonymous instance of AsyncTask and then executes that instance.

As described in Chapter 3, this will cause the AsyncTask method doInBackground to run on a background thread. In the AsyncTaskService, the anonymous AsyncTask's doInBackground method in turn calls the Service method executeTask.

What does this accomplish? Well, the Service method executeTask is now nearly identical to onStartCommand except that it is running on the AsyncTask's worker thread. It is now an excellent place to execute a long-running task.

It gets better. The call to the Service method onStartCommand has a side effect: It causes the framework to mark the Service as "started." This announces to the Android framework that this process is doing useful work. The framework, in response, will keep the priority of the process hosting the started Service higher than that of a process that is idle. Because of this, the AsyncTask running in this Service has a much better chance of running to completion than the same task running in a process within an Activity that is no longer visible.

The Android framework can easily tell when an Activity is no longer needed. When it is no longer visible, it is no longer doing useful work. There is no analogous way of knowing that a started Service is no longer useful. Once a Service is marked as started, it stays "started" until it is explicitly stopped. In order to be a good neighbor—releasing resources when they are not being used—either the Service's client must call stopService or the Service must call its own method, stopSelf. These calls announce to the framework that the Service is done with useful work, thus telling the framework that it can reduce the priority of the hosting process.

The AsyncTaskService manages its state by maintaining a count of running tasks. It increments the count when a new Intent arrives in onStartCommand, and decrements it again in the AsyncTask method onPostExecute when a task completes. Because both of these methods run on the main thread, there is no need to synchronize access to the counter. When the counter reaches 0, the Service calls stopSelf to declare to the framework that it is no longer doing useful work and that instance can be destroyed and the host process priority lowered.

> **Note**
>
> Listing 6.5 and the discussion around it are intended only as an example. The code is not complete. It will, for instance, miscount aborted tasks.

AsyncTaskService has exactly the features we've been looking for in a background execution mechanism. It runs tasks on a worker thread and it adjusts process priority to reduce the chance that the Android framework will interrupt useful background work. Furthermore, in the isolated environment of a Service, far from the UI machinery, there is much less chance of accidentally sharing state across threads.

A Service that provides all these features seems like a valuable thing. Android's designers realized the importance of such a tool and, in API level 3, Cupcake, introduced the IntentService—a service with very similar functionality—into the Android library.

An IntentService behaves almost exactly as does the AsyncTaskService, though it is implemented a bit differently. It runs tasks in its canonical method onHandleIntent, on a background thread. Like the AsyncTaskService, it declares itself not sticky, so that Intents are delivered to onHandleIntent only once and are not null. The one very significant difference is that instead of being powered by an AsyncTask and the ThreadPoolExecutor that backs them, the IntentService is powered by a single, private Looper and its worker thread.

There are several consequences to this. The first is that tasks that run on the worker thread of an IntentService can share state. Since they are all guaranteed to run on the very same thread, no state is being shared between threads. Clearly, the Service lifecycle methods, onCreate, onStartCommand, onDestroy, and so on, all of which are run on the main thread, must be careful not to share state with the tasks. The tasks themselves, though, are free to share with each other, without concern.

More significant, though, is that tasks execute in order in an IntentService. As each new Intent appears in a call to onStartCommand, it is enqueued on the Looper's message queue, eventually dequeued in order, and presented on the background thread as an argument to the onHandleIntent method. Only after that method processes the Intent to completion and returns, can the next Intent be dequeued for a subsequent call to onHandleIntent.

As noted in the discussion of AsyncTasks, sequential execution is frequently an advantage. It is much easier to reason about groups of sequential tasks than about tasks that are all mutually asynchronous. Conceptually, for instance, just because network tasks can happen out of order, with respect to UI tasks, network and UI tasks need not happen out of order with respect to each other. Indeed, the network task that logs a user in to her account must happen before the task that downloads her data. Allowing those things to happen out of order is not an advantage.

Architectures using multiple IntentServices for different classes of task, asynchronous with respect to one another but internally sequential, make a lot of sense. An IntentService is, however, not the right tool for an architecture that requires completely asynchronous task execution. A custom Service modeled on the AsyncTaskService, however, might be.

IntentServices are frequently called via static methods that are part of the Service class. These methods typically take as arguments a Context and any parameters that need to be passed to the task. They marshal the parameters into an Intent and then call startService, passing the new Intent. Both of the common IDEs, Eclipse and Android Studio, will generate this idiom from a code template. The static methods hide the details of Intent construction from the client and provide a fairly elegant way of invoking Service functionality—as elegant as any static reference can be. Listing 6.6 is an example of such a helper method.

Listing 6.6 **An Intent Service Helper Method**

```
public class CookieService extends IntentService {
  // ...

  private static final String ACTION_EAT
    = "net.callmeike.android.samplesvc.svc.action.EAT";
  private static final String EXTRA_PARAM_COOKIE
    = "net.callmeike.android.samplesvc.svc.extra.COOKIE";

  // ...

  public static void startActionDoIt(Context ctxt, String cookie) {
    Intent intent = new Intent(context, SampleService.class);
    intent.setAction(ACTION_EAT);
    intent.putExtra(EXTRA_PARAM_COOKIE, cookie);
    context.startService(intent);
```

```
  }

  // ...
}
```

Probably the most significant constraint on the IntentService is how difficult it is for it to return a result. While the Intent that starts the Service can carry, with some restrictions, task parameters, it is not immediately obvious how the IntentService might return a result. The typical Android solution, of course, is some kind of callback. In this case, perhaps this could be accomplished using a Handler to pass the result back to the main thread and then invoking a method on a passed callback handler from there. Hold that thought for the discussion of **messengers** later on.

Bound Services

Bound services have several appealing features. Within a single process, calls to the object managed by a bound Service are several orders of magnitude faster than sending Intents to an IntentService. Also, with a bound Service, it is much easier to create a bi-directional API: one in which methods return values. Their most important feature, though, is that the managed objects returned by Services can run not just on another thread, but also in another process.

Bound Services are among the most complex things that an Android application developer will ever encounter. For a moment, let's continue to gloss over most of that complexity and explore a very simplistic bound service client.

As previously noted, a bound Service looks at first like a factory for a managed object. Some closer examination, though, will reveal that this model is only partially accurate.

A Simple Bound Service

Recall from Figure 6.2 that a client initiates the binding process by calling the Context method `bindService`. In that call, it passes an Intent that identifies the target Service and a reference to a callback handler, an instance of `ServiceConnection`. It also passes some flags (to be explored later). Listing 6.7 shows the code.

Listing 6.7   **A Simple Bound Service Client**

```
public class SimpleActivity
  extends AppCompatActivity
  implements ServiceConnection
{
  @Override
  public void onServiceConnected(ComponentName name, IBinder binder) {
    setService(((LocalService.ServiceBinder) binder).getService());
  }
```

```
  @Override
  public void onServiceDisconnected(ComponentName name) {
    setService(null);
  }

  @Override
  protected void onStart() {
    super.onStart();
    bindService(
      new Intent(this, LocalService.class),
      this,
      BIND_AUTO_CREATE);
  }

  @Override
  protected void onStop() {
    super.onStop();
    setService(null);
    unbindService(this);
  }

  // ...

  private void setService(LocalService svc) {
    service = svc;
    addButton.setEnabled(svc != null);
  }
}
```

If the Android framework cannot successfully deliver the parameter Intent to some Service, the call to bindService returns a boolean false. This could happen either because the Intent does not match any Service registered with the system or because the system fails to start the application containing the registered Service. If bindService returns false, the binding process is aborted.

If the system succeeds in locating a bindable service, the call to bindService returns true. Asynchronously, the target Service receives a copy of the Intent sent by the bindService call, as the parameter to a call to its onBind method. The onBind method eventually returns an object, and the Android framework, again asynchronously, delivers it (or, at least, something very similar) as the parameter to a call to the onServiceConnected method of the callback handler (the second argument to the bindService call).

Just as with the IntentService, application code that binds a Service is responsible for releasing unused resources when it is done with them and assuring that the Service is unbound when it is no longer needed. The client unbinds the Service by calling the Context method unbindService and passing the callback handler that was used to bind it. If it is the last client to unbind—if there are no other bound clients—the framework calls the Service's onUnbind method.

Binding A Service

Client code must be able to construct an Intent that names the Service it wants to target. As previously mentioned, post Marshmallow, API 23, the client code must know, at the very least, the exact package name for the application containing that Service. In addition, it must know how to match the target Service's IntentFilter if there is one. If the target Service has not declared an IntentFilter, the client must know the exact name of the class that implements the Service.

In support of this requirement, many developers that create Services meant for public use document the Service API in a file called a **contract**. A contract is a Java source file that defines symbols for the constants necessary to use a Service. The file must not contain references to application-internal symbols or types. It can be distributed independently, perhaps as a web site download or via e-mail.

Client applications include the contract file in their source and use the symbols it defines—and, hopefully, the documentation it provides—to interact with the public Service correctly. Android documentation recommends using a contract to publish the interface to a ContentProvider. They are equally useful for publishing bindable Service APIs.

The contract is a good idea for a far more significant reason. Notice that the onServiceConnected method—the method called to deliver the Service-managed object to the client—takes as a parameter an object of type IBinder. This is the beginning of the divergence between the Service API and the standard Factory pattern.

Unlike most Java implementations of the Factory pattern, Services are neither synchronous nor type-safe. The client receives the instance of the Service-managed object as a callback, not as the return from the call to the factory method. Furthermore, the Service onBind method returns a Binder object and the client receives an IBinder. It is the client's responsibility to know exactly what kind of object to expect and to cast the IBinder it receives to the correct Java type.

An improvement on the Service-as-factory metaphor is suggested by the way that the Service onBind method is called. Between the time an instance of a given Service is created and the time it is destroyed, its onBind method is called only once for all Intents that are equals in the Java sense.

For example, all explicit Intents that target some given Service are equal—they all contain the name of the same package and the name of the same class within that package. Because they are the same, only the first attempt to bind a Service with an explicit Intent will produce a call to the Service's onBind method.

Subsequent calls to bindService do not cause onBind to be called again. Instead, the Android framework simply returns the object obtained from the first call to onBind. Perhaps a Service is more like a lazy singleton than a factory.

> **Note**
>
> An architectural anti-pattern that was common in enterprise software around the turn of the century involved systems built out of large singletons, frequently called "Managers." Such systems were monolithic and object-oriented in name only. They were difficult to test and abandoned any advantages that O-O programming might provide.
>
> Steve Yegge wrote an excellent and funny essay about singletons and the architectures they inspire in his blog at https://sites.google.com/site/steveyegge2/singleton-considered-stupid.
>
> If you were a developer during that era, the discussion of Android's Services might make you architecturally uncomfortable.

Unbinding A Service

Even the Service-as-a-singleton model, though, does not hold up. It collapses with the discovery of the `unbindService` method. Singletons are not usually subject to destruction. The very existence of the `unbindService` method is curious and requires closer examination.

First, note that `bindService` and `unbindService` are stateful methods on an instance of the type `Context`. When a Service is bound, the binding Context remembers the binding. Only that Context can unbind that connection. The code in Listing 6.8, for instance, generates the following error:

```
...
java.lang.IllegalArgumentException: Service not registered:
  net.callmeike.android.servicedemo.MainActivity@6ccc2eb
...
```

Listing 6.8   Unbinding from the Wrong Context

```
@Override
protected void onStart() {
  super.onStart();
  bindService(new Intent(this, LocalService.class), con, BIND_AUTO_CREATE);
}

@Override
protected void onStop() {
  super.onStop();
  getApplicationContext().unbindService(con); // !!! ERROR!
}
```

The problem is that the `bindService` method, in Listing 6.8, is called on the Activity, which is a Context. The `unbindService` method, however, is called on the application context. The application context is, surely, a Context but it is not the same object as the Activity. The application context has no record of the connection so the attempt to unbind fails.

There is an interesting corollary that arises when an Activity binds a Service. Because the binding belongs to a particular Context—an Activity—and because the framework controls the lifecycle of that Context, it knows when it destroys the Activity that any binding that has not been unbound can never be unbound correctly. When an Activity is destroyed without unbinding a Service that it has bound, the framework generates an error message like this:

```
...
Activity net.callmeike.android.servicesandbox.MainActivity has leaked
   ServiceConnection net.callmeike.android.servicesandbox.MainActivity@1d77f05
   that was originally bound here
...
```

Binding a Service affects the priority of the process that hosts the Service. The framework expects a component that binds a Service to manage that binding explicitly and to unbind it when it is no longer needed. If it does not, the framework signals an error.

The most important thing about the `unbindService` method, though, is that it probably has no immediate effect on the object whose reference was passed to the client in its `onService-Connected` method. One might reasonably expect that unbinding a Service—particularly if that Service is in a remote process—would sever the connection to the remote object. It does not.

This leads to yet another analogy for a bound Service. A bound Service is like a Java `SoftReference` to a singleton. When the Service is bound, the framework promises to notify the client whenever it makes a change in the reference. When it sets the reference to point to a valid object, it calls `onServiceConnected`. When it sets the reference to `null`, it calls `onServiceDisconnected`.

When the Service is no longer bound to a callback handler, however, the framework is not under any obligation to notify anyone. The reference provided by the Service does not become invalid. The framework might make it invalid, though, without notifying the client.

When no client is listening to changes in the Service status, the framework assumes that no one cares about it. When clients are listening for changes in status, the framework assumes that the Service is doing work on their behalf and that the Service should not be destroyed unless it is necessary. If it must destroy the Service, it notifies the clients and tries to recreate the Service as soon as possible. Just as an Activity is considered useless if no one can see it, though, bound Services are considered useless if no one is bound to them. The Service object can be destroyed and the host priority lowered.

Binding Multiple Services

Unlike many of the other callback handlers in the Android universe (`View.onClickHandler`, `LoaderManager.LoaderCallbacks`), a `ServiceConnection` can manage only a single binding. Using the Context that binds the Service (often an Activity) as the callback handler, as illustrated in Listing 6.7, is a common idiom. It is an idiom, though, that enables binding only a single Service connection. Connecting to multiple Services requires multiple callback handlers, as shown in Listing 6.9.

Listing 6.9   **Binding Multiple Services to a Single Context**

```
public class Bind2Activity extends AppCompatActivity {
  private ServiceConnection con1 = new ServiceConnection() {
    @Override
    public void onServiceConnected(ComponentName name, IBinder binder) {
      svc1 = (((LocalService1.ServiceBinder) binder).getService());
    }

    @Override
    public void onServiceDisconnected(ComponentName name) {
      svc1 = null;
    }
  }

  private ServiceConnection con2 = new ServiceConnection() {
    @Override
    public void onServiceConnected(ComponentName name, IBinder binder) {
      svc2 = (((LocalService2.ServiceBinder) binder).getService());
    }

    @Override
    public void onServiceDisconnected(ComponentName name) {
      svc2 = null;
    }
  }

  // ...

  @Override
  protected void onCreate(Bundle savedInstanceState) {
    super.onCreate(savedInstanceState);
    setContentView(R.layout.activity_main2);

    bindService(
      new Intent(this, LocalService1.class),
      con1,
      BIND_AUTO_CREATE)
    bindService(
      new Intent(this, LocalService2.class),
      con2,
      BIND_AUTO_CREATE)
  }

  // ...
}
```

Service Lifecycle

The end of the Service-as-a-singleton metaphor comes with the realization that a Service requires careful cooperation from its clients to prevent them from getting more than one copy of the object it manages.

The Android framework calls the onBind method of a Service only once during the lifetime of an instance of that Service, for each equivalent Intent. On the other hand, the lifetime of the Service object is, from the point of view of its client, nearly random. Different instances of a single Service can easily return different managed objects.

Consider the minimal Service in Listing 6.10. The MinimalService returns a new instance of its managed object ManagedObject, for each call to onBind. Because onBind is called only once for the explicit Intent used to bind MinimalService, one might be forgiven for thinking that ManagedObject was a singleton.

Listing 6.10   **Minimal Bound Service**

```
public class MinimalService extends Service {

  @Override
  public IBinder onBind(Intent intent) {
    return new ManagedObject();
  }
}
```

It is not. As Figure 6.3 illustrates, a client can quite easily end up with references to two distinct instances of the managed object.

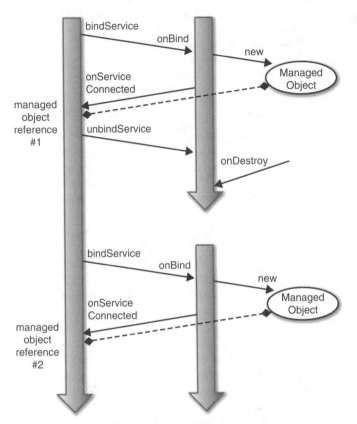

Figure 6.3   Service-managed objects are not singletons

The client's second call to bindService in Figure 6.3 happens to be forwarded to a different instance of the Service from the first. The framework does not have a cached instance of the managed object—it was cleared when the Service was destroyed—so it calls through to onBind.

The onBind method creates a new object and returns it. The client that incorrectly did not forget the first instance of the managed object when it unbound the Service, now receives a reference to a second instance. Clearly, the client code has a bug. Nonetheless, it now holds two references to distinct "singletons."

Of course, in addition, there are lifecycles. Even after repairing the code in Listing 6.10 so that the managed object is a singleton (shown in Listing 6.11), expecting singleton-like behavior can still lead to surprises.

Listing 6.11 **Singleton Bound Service**

```
public class SingletonService extends Service {
  private static ManagedObject managedObject;
  private static int counter;

  @Override
  public IBinder onBind(Intent intent) {
    if (null == managedObject) {
      managedObject = new ManagedObject(++counter);
    }
    return managedObject;
  }
}
```

This code is attempting to count the number of instances of ManageObject created by the Service. It is entirely possible, though, that a client will see that count suddenly drop from some large number to 1.

If the Service process is stopped and restarted, even its static variables are reinitialized. When a client and a Service are in different processes, the Service can lose all its state, even though the client does not.

When a client is bound to a Service and the Service must be killed, the framework restarts the Service as soon as it has an opportunity to do so. The client will receive first a call to onServiceDisconnected and then a call to onServiceConnected. In the case of the SingletonService in Listing 6.11, regardless of what the value of counter had been previously, it will now be 1.

It turns out that Services are just not a precise match for any common architectural pattern. Using them correctly requires understanding them and their specific, unique behavior.

Priorities and Flags

The flags supplied as the third argument to the call to bindService are an incomprehensible hairball. They fall, more or less, into three categories: those that affect the connection process, those that affect the priority of the process that hosts the bound Service, and WTF. The flags are a bitset and so can be OR-ed together. Specifying more than one flag from each of the three groups, though, is probably not very meaningful.

In the first category, a flag that affects the connection process is the most important flag of all, BIND_AUTO_CREATE. Nearly every call to bindService should specify this flag.

When specified, this flag tells the framework to start the host process if it is not already running, to create an instance of the Service class if none exists, and to call the onBind method of the now-running instance.

It can be amusing to consider what happens when bindSerive is called without the BIND_AUTO_CREATE flag. Even when the call to bindService returns true (indicating that the framework has successfully located a Service to which to bind) there might be no subsequent call to the callback handler. Milliseconds, seconds, minutes, even hours can go by without a call to the callback handler.

Suppose, though, that for some reason, hours hence, other code makes a call to `startService` with an Intent targeting the same Service. Because an instance of the Service is created and started in response to that call, the binding client's callback handler will, hours after it called `bindService`, suddenly receive the connection. This is so weird that it seems inevitable that someone will find a problem to which it is the perfect solution.

In the WTF category is the `BIND_DEBUG_UNBIND` flag.

The remaining flags `BIND_NOT_FOREGROUND`, `BIND_ABOVE_CLIENT`, `BIND_ALLOW_OOM_MANAGEMENT`, `BIND_WAIVE_PRIORITY`, `BIND_IMPORTANT`, and `BIND_ADJUST_WITH_ACTIVITY` all control the priority of the process hosting the bound Service. With the exception of `BIND_NOT_FOREGROUND`, they were all introduced in API 14, Ice Cream Sandwich. While the documentation describes them in some detail, their exact meanings are complex and quite difficult to uncover.

A Local Bound Service

Before moving on to the discussion of inter-process communication there is one more subject to address. It is, perhaps, slightly out of order to introduce here an optimization for inter-process communication before discussing IPC itself. It is an important optimization, however, and describing it here will keep it from interrupting the discussion of IPC to come.

Process boundaries have been largely ignored so far in this chapter. None of the illustrations include them. None of the code mentions them. The obvious assumption—true for most applications in general and even most of the code in most Android applications—is that everything is running in a single process. That is not the case for the Services. Most of the discussion and code in this chapter applies, whether the Service and its client are in the same or different processes. Services are nearly blind to process borders.

Just for a moment, though, consider a Service that is known to be hosted in the same process as its client. In this constrained case, there is a trick that can be used to eliminate most of the overhead of communication with the Service-managed object that is imposed by the IPC framework. It is slightly unfortunate that a Service—the tool for blurring the distinction between in- and out-of-process communication—is often used in a way that constrains it to a single process. The trick, however, has such a dramatic effect on performance that within a process, a developer would be crazy not to use it. Listing 6.12 demonstrates the trick.

Listing 6.12 **Local Service**

```
public class LocalService extends Service {
  public class ServiceBinder extends Binder {
    public LocalService getService() { return LocalService.this; }
  }
```

```
@Override
public IBinder onBind(Intent intent) {
  return new ServiceBinder();
}

public Foo doSomething(Bar bar) {
  // …
}
}
```

The inner class, ServiceBinder, has two essential attributes. Since it extends Binder, it implements the IBinder interface and can be returned by the onBind method. A Binder is a large, heavyweight object that implements IBinder and has many super powers. In this particular case, though, those powers are all pretty much irrelevant. Because the Service and its client are in the same process, the client callback handler will receive, as the argument to its onServiceConnected method, exactly the object that onBind returns. Note that this is *not* the case when the client and the Service are in separate processes!

Because ServiceBinder is an inner class of LocalService, it holds a reference to the Service. That's just Java. It can expose that reference and does so in its getService method. When the client receives the callback, it simply casts the passed IBinder parameter as the LocalService.ServiceBinder it knows it to be and then calls the getService method. It now holds a reference to the LocalService object. Listing 6.13 demonstrates a LocalService client.

Listing 6.13 **Local Service Client**

```
private LocalService service;

// ...

@Override
public void onServiceConnected(ComponentName name, IBinder binder) {
  service = ((LocalService.ServiceBinder) binder).getService();
}

// ...
```

This is an idiom. In the most common expression of this idiom, exemplified in Listing 6.12, the Binder that is passed between the onBind and onServiceConnected methods holds a reference to the Service itself. That's just because it is easy to do. The Service is not only the factory for the managed object, but also the managed object that the factory returns.

This is by no means necessary, and it can make testing quite difficult. Constructing unit tests for the client-visible methods on the LocalService, for instance, requires mocking a Service.

That will make it difficult to run the tests except in an environment that can instantiate a Service: an Android device, or perhaps Robolectric.

The `ServiceBinder`, however, can return any object it wants. A more reasonable take on this idiom is that the `ServiceBinder`'s `getService` method returns a reference to an object that has been injected into the Service using one of the IOC frameworks. Listing 6.14 is an example of this technique, using Dagger2.

Listing 6.14 **Service Injection**

```
public class LocalService extends Service {
  public class ServiceBinder extends Binder {
    private final ServiceProvider provider;
    ServiceBinder(ServiceProvider provider) { this.provider = provider; }
    public ServiceProvider getService() { return provider; }
  }

  private static ServiceBinder serviceBinder;


  @Inject ServiceProvider provider;

  @Override
  public void onCreate() {
    super.onCreate();
    if (serviceBinder == null) {
      DaggerProviderComponent.create().inject(this);
      serviceBinder = new ServiceBinder(provider);
    }
  }

  @Override
  public IBinder onBind(Intent intent) {
    return serviceBinder;
  }
}
```

Inter-Process Communication

This chapter has alluded several times to the fact that a Service can run in a completely different process from it client, and that the Service is Android's tool for inter-process communication. The entire discussion of Services is just the groundwork for understanding how to execute a task that is not just on a different thread, but in a different process.

Java's standard for inter-process communication is the `Serializable` interface. Android supports Java serialization but introduces a new and simpler contract, `Parcelable`, for objects that it must serialize. In addition to the `Parcelable` interface, the Android tools suite includes a compiler for Android's inter-process communication language, Android Interface Definition Language (AIDL).

Figure 6.4 illustrates the Android IPC mechanism.

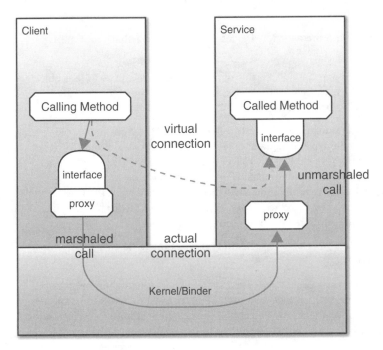

Figure 6.4   Binder IPC

Like most IPC mechanisms, Android's is divided conceptually into two pieces, a client side and a server side. These two sides are called, respectively, the **proxy** and the **stub**. The client thinks that it is talking to an instance of some object. It obtained this object from a factory, though, and the factory slyly returned, not an instance of the required object, but a proxy to it. The proxy looks as much as possible like the remote object. In Java terms, that probably means that it implements the same interface.

Instead of actually containing the implementation code, the proxy's responsibility is to marshal calls into messages. The messages are transferred to the remote process. In Android, this transfer is handled by a module in the Linux kernel, called Binder.

Binder copies the marshaled message into the target process's memory space, where it hands it to the stub. It is the stub's job to unmarshal the message and make a call to the actual implementation of the object: the thing that the client thought it was calling.

If the call returns a value, the process takes place in reverse to transfer the return value back to the client.

Parcelables

A Parcelable object is an object that implements s specific API. To begin, it must implement the `Parcelable` interface. That interface requires the implementation of two methods, `describeContents` and `writeToParcel`. In addition, a Parcelable object must have, *exactly*, a public static member named `CREATOR`, that is an implementation of `Parcelable.Creator` for the Parcelable type.

The `writeToParcel` method and the `CREATOR` are, respectively, the marshaler and unmarshaler.

When the framework needs to marshal a Parcelable object, it holds a reference to that object. It simply calls the object's `writeToParcel` method, passing a `Parcel`. The object is responsible for marshaling its state into the passed Parcel.

When the framework needs to unmarshal from a Parcel, it reads tokens from the Parcel. A token in the Parcel identifies the type of the next object to be unmarshaled. From that token, the framework can identify the Java class of the object to be unmarshaled. Since `CREATOR` is a public static member of the class, the unmarshaler can easily obtain a reference to a `Parcelable.Creator` for the object to be unmarshaled. The framework calls the Creator's `createFromParcel` method passing the Parcel. The Creator is responsible for reading the previously marshaled state from the Parcel and returning a new object.

The Android documentation on Parcelables is clear and fairly complete. There are a few tips, however, that can be useful.

First, the usual implementation of `createFromParcel` is a call to a constructor. In order to keep the marshaling and unmarshaling code near each other, many developers use a special package-protected constructor that takes the Parcel as its only argument. Others favor reading the Parcel in the `createFromParcel` method, and then calling a constructor that completely specifies object state.

Next, developers might find it surprising that state is unmarshaled from a Parcel in the same order in which it was marshaled. If `writeToParcel` writes a `String` and then an `int`, `createFromParcel` will read a `String` and then an `int`.

Finally, although the Parcelable API makes marshaling and unmarshaling Parcelables very fast (typically about twice as fast as Java Serialization on the Android platform), it makes them nearly impossible to sub-class. Architecting a cross-process API that minimizes the need for inheritance in Parcelables will prevent many headaches.

Messengers

Android's Messenger class has come up twice already. Messengers are the reason for the remote fields in the Message class, described in the "Gory Details" section of Chapter 5, "Loopers and Handlers." They are also the way of returning a result from an IntentService alluded to previously in this chapter.

A Messenger is, essentially, a Parcelable reference to a Handler. A Handler enables an external thread to enqueue a Message for a Looper's worker thread. A Messenger extends that capability, enabling code to pass a reference to a Handler anywhere that it can pass a Parcelable. In particular, passing a Messenger in an Intent, for example, enables the recipient of the Intent, possibly in a different process, to enqueue Messages for local processing. Listing 6.15 illustrates.

Listing 6.15   **Using a Messenger**

```java
public class MessengerServiceHelper {
  public interface MessengerCallbacks { void onComplete(String val); }

  public static final String SERVICE_PACKAGE
    = "net.callmeike.android.messengersandbox";
  public static final String ACTION_SEND
    = "net.callmeike.android.messengersandbox.svc.action.SEND";
  public static final String EXTRA_PARAM_BASE
    = "net.callmeike.android.messengersandbox.svc.extra.BASE";
  public static final String EXTRA_PARAM_MESSENGER
    = "net.callmeike.android.messengersandbox.svc.extra.MESSENGER";
  public static final String EXTRA_RESPONSE
    = "net.callmeike.android.messengersandbox.svc.extra.RESPONSE";

  public static final int WHAT_REPLY = -1;

  public static void startActionSend(
    Context context,
    String base,
    final MessengerCallbacks callbacks)
  {
    Messenger messenger = new Messenger(new Handler(Looper.myLooper()) {
      @Override
      public void handleMessage(Message msg) {
        switch (msg.what) {
          case WHAT_REPLY:
            Bundle resp = (Bundle) msg.obj;
            callbacks.onComplete(resp.getString(EXTRA_RESPONSE, ""));
            break;
          default:
            super.handleMessage(msg);
        }
      }
    });

    Intent intent = new Intent();
    intent.setPackage(SERVICE_PACKAGE);
    intent.setAction(ACTION_SEND);
```

```
      intent.putExtra(EXTRA_PARAM_BASE, base);
      intent.putExtra(EXTRA_PARAM_MESSENGER, messenger);
      context.startService(intent);
    }
}
```

Consider a client in one application that wants to use the MessengerService, which is part of an entirely separate application called net.callmeike.android.messengersandbox. It does so by creating an instance of the MessengerServiceHelper and calling its method startActionSend.

The magic is in startActionSend. It creates a Messenger wrapping a Handler for the thread on which the method is called (Looper.myLooper), adds it to an Intent, and then launches the Intent.

The MessengerService is shown in Listing 6.16. It receives the Intent sent by the helper method as a parameter to the call of its onHandleIntent method, retrieves the two parameters that the helper method included, and calls handleActionSend with them.

Listing 6.16 **A Messenger Service**

```java
public class MessengerService extends IntentService {
  private static final String TAG = "MessengerSvc";

  public MessengerService() {
    super(TAG);
  }

  @Override
  protected void onHandleIntent(Intent intent) {
    if (intent == null) { return; }

    final String action = intent.getAction();
    switch (action) {
      case MessengerServiceHelper.ACTION_SEND:
        handleActionSend(
          intent.getStringExtra(
            MessengerServiceHelper.EXTRA_PARAM_BASE),
          (Messenger) intent.getParcelableExtra(
            MessengerServiceHelper.EXTRA_PARAM_MESSENGER));
        break;
      default:
        Log.i(TAG, "unexpected action: " + action);
    }
  }

  private void handleActionSend(String base, Messenger messenger) {
```

```
    Bundle resp = new Bundle();
    resp.putString(MessengerServiceHelper.EXTRA_RESPONSE, base + " roundtrip!");
    try {
      messenger.send(
        Message.obtain(null, MessengerServiceHelper.WHAT_REPLY, resp));
    }
    catch (RemoteException e) {
      Log.e(TAG, "reply failed: ", e);
    }
  }
}
```

handleActionSend performs its task (the trivial task of concatenating the word "roundtrip" to the passed string, in this case), and then prepares to return its result. Returning the result should recall Chapter 5: the code obtains a Message from the pool, and then uses the passed Messenger to enqueue it for processing by a Looper.

There is one detail here that is worthy of note. Unlike the Handlers in Chapter 5, this Messenger is about to send a Message between processes. It must be able to marshal and unmarshal the object that it sends. It follows, therefore, that if the Message field obj contains a reference to an object, that object must be Parcelable. In fact, the Messenger method send verifies this by checking the type of the object to which obj refers.

In the example, the return value is a String. Although a String is one of the primitively parcelable types, it does not implement Parcelable. An attempt to send a String with a Messenger will fail with a message like this:

```
E/AndroidRuntime: FATAL EXCEPTION: IntentService[MessengerSvc]
Process: net.callmeike.android.messengersandbox:service, PID: 2106
java.lang.RuntimeException:
    Can't marshal non-Parcelable objects across processes.
```

As the example demonstrates, though, avoiding this error is trivial. Android's Bundle type does extend Parcelable, and it knows how to marshal a String. Simply wrapping the return value in a Bundle fixes the problem.

Returning to Listing 6.15, the Message sent from the Service is dequeued back in the client process and passed as the argument to a call to the Handler's handleMessage method. That method parses the message and calls the previously registered callback handler with the result.

As nifty as this is, do not let it cause you to forget the lifecycle problem. If the passed callback Handler is a reference to an Activity, for instance, that Activity cannot be released for garbage collection until the Handler to which it refers, is collected. That happens only after the Message that refers to it is removed from the Looper queue. If the Activity has been destroyed before that, of course, the Activity can be in an inconsistent state and the call to onComplete can explode.

Using AIDL

AIDL, Android Interface Definition Language, is the next step up from simple Parcelables. It supports Java-like method calls and return values over the Binder IPC mechanism. AIDL is a multifeatured language, and a complete discussion of it is out of the scope of this book. It is described in detail in the Android documentation. What follows is an introduction.

The AIDL compiler is an instance of a tool that is very common in IPC mechanisms. Its job is to generate the Java code that implements both a proxy and a stub, given a single interface specification. The AIDL language, the source language for the AIDL compiler, looks a lot like Java.

Using AIDL to communicate with an object managed by a Service running in another process is a multistep process.

1. **Define the interface:** Listing 6.17 show a simple AIDL definition. Note that clients of a Service with an AIDL-defined API need the Java classes for the API. They can get them by compiling shared AIDL, compiling shared Java code, or by using a library containing the compiled API types. A Service with a public interface must publish its API in one of those three ways. It makes sense to put the API into a separate, sharable module, perhaps along with the contract.

Listing 6.17　**A Simple AIDL Definition**

```
package net.callmeike.android.servicesandbox.svc;

interface ILogger {
  void startLogging();
  void stopLogging();
}
```

2. **Compile the interface:** It is instructive to examine the compiled output. Gradle, the standard build tool for Android, puts the compiled AIDL output into the directory `<builddirectory>/generated/source/aidl/<variant>/<classpath>/<interface>`. For instance, the `ILogger` AIDL definition in Listing 6.17, built for the debug variant of its application, is in the file `.../generated/source/aidl/debug/net/callmeike/servicesandbox/service/svc/ILogger.java`.

   Listing 6.18 shows annotated excerpts of the AIDL output. Perhaps surprisingly, a single Java source file is the implementation of both the proxy and the stub.

Listing 6.18　**AIDL-Generated Code**

```
package net.callmeike.android.servicesandbox.svc;

public interface ILogger extends android.os.IInterface
{
  // The service side extends this Stub
```

```
public static abstract class Stub
  extends android.os.Binder
  implements net.callmeike.android.servicesandbox.svc.ILogger
{

 // Code elided ...

  @Override public boolean onTransact(
    int code,
    android.os.Parcel data,
    android.os.Parcel reply,
    int flags)
    throws android.os.RemoteException
  {
    switch (code)
    {
      // when this opcode appears in the stream,
      // call the implementation of startLogging
      case TRANSACTION_startLogging:
      {
        data.enforceInterface(DESCRIPTOR);
        this.startLogging();
        reply.writeNoException();
        return true;
      }

      // Code elided ...

    }
    return super.onTransact(code, data, reply, flags);
  }

  // The client makes calls to this proxy
  private static class Proxy
    implements net.callmeike.android.servicesandbox.svc.ILogger
  {
    // the proxy has a stream to the remote
    private android.os.IBinder mRemote;
    Proxy(android.os.IBinder remote)
    {
      mRemote = remote;
    }

    //  ... code elided

    // a call to the startLogging method
    // marshals the arguments into the stream
```

```
@Override public void startLogging() throws android.os.RemoteException
{
  android.os.Parcel _data = android.os.Parcel.obtain();
  android.os.Parcel _reply = android.os.Parcel.obtain();
  try {
    _data.writeInterfaceToken(DESCRIPTOR);
    mRemote.transact(Stub.TRANSACTION_startLogging, _data, _reply, 0);
    _reply.readException();
  }
  finally {
    _reply.recycle();
    _data.recycle();
  }
}

// ... code elided

}

// here are the definitions of the opcodes
static final int TRANSACTION_startLogging
  = (android.os.IBinder.FIRST_CALL_TRANSACTION + 0);
static final int TRANSACTION_stopLogging
  = (android.os.IBinder.FIRST_CALL_TRANSACTION + 1);
}

// here is the interface that the proxy and the implementation implement
public void startLogging() throws android.os.RemoteException;
public void stopLogging() throws android.os.RemoteException;
}
```

3. **Implement the interface:** This is the actual implementation of the task. The important part is the first line, the definition of the class. It must extend the AIDL-generated stub, which in turn implements the AIDL-defined interface and extends Binder, the IPC mechanism. Listing 6.19 shows the implementation of a remote object.

Listing 6.19 **Sample Managed Object Implementation**

```
public class Logger extends ILogger.Stub {

  @Override
  public void startLogging() {
    // ...
  }
```

```
public void stopLogging() {
  // ...
  }
}
```

4. **Return the object from a Service:** Several listings in this chapter have demonstrated the process of returning a managed object from a bound Service. The Service must be declared in the manifest, must carefully create an instance of the managed object, and must return it from a call to onBind.

   Note that this time the object that the client receives in its onServiceConnected call is absolutely *not* the same object that the Service returned. It is, instead, a connection through Binder to the remote.

5. **Wrap the Binder connection in the proxy:** The client must have access to the same API definition used by the Service. Whereas when the client and service were both in the same process, the client simply cast the object that it received in the call to onServiceConnected, this time it wraps the passed reference, a Binder connection to the remote process, with the AIDL-generated stub using the asInterface method. The connection is now complete. Listing 6.20 is the implementation of a client to the Service shown in Listing 6.19.

Listing 6.20   **Using a Remote Managed Object**

```
private ILogger service;

public void onServiceConnected(ComponentName name, IBinder binder) {
  service = ILogger.Stub.asInterface(binder);
  button.setEnabled(true)
}

void startLogger() {
  service.startLogging();
}
```

Creating Processes

Running in a remote process has significant overhead. All that marshaling, unmarshaling, and copying across address spaces has a cost. Sometimes, though, that overhead is worth it. Just to pick one example, a remote task can crash horribly without affecting its client.

The most obvious way of running a task in a different process is by running it in a different application. This is simply a matter of using an Intent to address a Service that is part of that different application.

That works fine if target devices already have the required application installed. When an application must be responsible itself for arranging for multiple processes, requiring more than one application is cumbersome. Trying to get users to install a second app, for instance, simply to get the first one to work properly, is just too much friction.

> **Note**
>
> There is no requirement that an application have a UI. It is perfectly possible to create an application that consists of only one or more Services. Such an application will not appear on the Android Desktop and cannot by run explicitly by the user.
>
> It is even possible for such an application to contain an Activity, as long as that Activity does not have an Intent filter that matches action `android.intent.action.MAIN` and category `android.intent.category.LAUNCHER`.

A second way to create processes is in the application manifest, using the `android:process` component attribute. This attribute enables specifying that a component should be run in a process other than the default process for the application. Listing 6.21 is an example of a Service, run in a process named "net.callmeike.android.servicesandbox:other."

Listing 6.21 **Specifying a Component's Process**

```
<service
  android:name=".svc.SimpleService"
  android:exported="true"
  android:process=":other"
  >
  <intent-filter>
    <action android:name="net.callmeike.android.servicesandbox.LOGGER"/>
  </intent-filter>
  <intent-filter>
    <action android:name="net.callmeike.android.servicesandbox.BLOGGER"/>
  </intent-filter>
</service>
```

Android distinguishes two types of process, local and remote. A **local process** is a process whose name begins with a ":". Other applications with other package names cannot reproduce the name. If other application cannot name the process, they cannot use it in their process specifications and cannot put their components into it.

A **remote process**, on the other hand, has a name to which other applications have access. Remote names begin with a lower-case alpha character and must contain at least one "." character. If two different applications signed with the same certificate and running with the same Linux user ID specify the same process for components, those components will all run in the very same process.

Listing 6.22 is nearly identical to Listing 6.21, but puts SimpleService in a process into which another application could put components.

Listing 6.22 **Specifying a Component's Process**

```
<service
  android:name=".svc.SimpleService"
  android:exported="true"
  android:process=" com.callmeike.android.shared"
  >
  <intent-filter>
    <action android:name="net.callmeike.android.servicesandbox.LOGGER"/>
  </intent-filter>
  <intent-filter>
    <action android:name="net.callmeike.android.servicesandbox.BLOGGER"/>
  </intent-filter>
</service>
```

Binder, Considered Briefly

No discussion of Android inter-process communication would be complete without some consideration of Binder. In a very real sense, Binder is Android's heart. It enables Android's security mechanism, its unique cross-application component structure, and the very powerful mechanism for calling other applications as if they were functions.

Android's Binder is fourth-generation. The original Binder was developed for BeOS. It made an appearance at Palm, and was then published as OpenBinder. The Android version is a reimplementation. Every Android developer should be aware of Binder and have a basic understanding of its behavior.

Binder Threads

An Android remote process is just a different process. All of the normal Android scheduling and threading behavior applies. In particular, Service lifecycle methods are called, in a remote process, as they always are, from the process main thread. Methods on a Service managed object in the remote process, however, are called from Binder threads.

A Binder thread is a thread created explicitly for use by Binder. When requests from one or more remote client processes queue up for execution by a bound Service, the kernel requests that the Server process's framework spin up new threads to handle them. These new threads, once spun up, request work from the kernel.

An application will not spin up more than fifteen such threads. This is a software limit compiled into Android. While it is possible that this number will vary over time, or even from device vendor to device vendor, the mainline Android code has not changed this limit in the ten years of Android's existence.

Binder Data Transfer Limits

The memory buffer that Binder uses to transfer data is limited in size. Again, although the specifics will vary over time and vendor, the rule of thumb is that it is not possible to move more than 1MB in a single transaction.

There is a way around this, though. Because Binder is part of the kernel, it can refer to kernel private structures. Among such structures are open files. In much the way that a parent and a child process can have a reference to the same open file after a `fork` call, so can one process open a file and pass it through Binder to another. A client, passing a large image, to a Service, might open the image as a file, and pass the open file to the Service, instead of passing every single byte of the image, through Binder.

Binding to Death

It might occasionally be necessary for a Service to discover that a client has aborted. This is particularly important when the Service is managing scarce or expensive resources and cannot tolerate a client claiming them and then failing to release them.

When a connection between a Service and its client provides a way for the Service to call the client, the Service will hold an `IBinder` for the client call. The `IBinder` interface defines the method `linkToDeath`. By calling this method, the Service registers for a callback if the connection to the client fails.

This is possible because Binder is part of the kernel. The kernel does not monitor the states of processes; it is the thing that creates those processes. No heartbeat or polling is required. The kernel is guaranteed to know if the client process fails. Binder passes the information to the registered callback.

Summary

Although architecturally they are a kind of a catch-all for functionality that has no other home, Services are an essential tool for the developer. They are the only way in the Android environment of adjusting process priority while doing valuable work that is not visible in the UI. The two kinds of Service, started and bound, provide a narrower and a broader interface, respectively, for tasks run not only on separate threads, but in separate processes.

7

Periodic Tasks

The great enemy of communication, we find, is the illusion of it.

William H. Whyte

One of the most important varieties of asynchronous task is a task that must repeat on a schedule. Scheduled tasks usually synchronize the state of the application that contains them with some external state. Of course, whenever possible, it is better if the external state pushes change notification to the application: push notifications don't have granularity lag and scale better than polling.

Sometime, however, polling and explicit scheduling are necessary. An application that depends on a resource that doesn't send push notifications is going to have to poll that resource. Alternatively, sometimes conditions local to the device drive explicit scheduling. An application that needs to perform an operation that should only take place when the device is connected to a power source or an unmetered network might have to schedule that operation for another time when the required conditions are in effect.

Task Characteristics

The general category of "Repeating" or "Scheduled" tasks is overly broad. It contains things like the screen refresh every 17ms or so, and recharging the device battery every day or so. Both of these things are interesting and can be important to understand when building a responsive, resource-thrifty application. This chapter, however, focuses on a more specific set of tasks.

The tasks considered here are a single code path, executed multiple times. They have a period that is somewhere between one minute and one day. These are the things that an application schedules, as part of its business logic, to synchronize itself with its environment. Some examples might be recording waypoints when tracking a runner's path, pushing new photos to a remote server, or polling a third-party web site for updates. Not included are the tasks executed when new media is mounted or when loading images from a remote source for display in a long, fast-moving list view.

Even this constrained list includes things that are hard to do well. The usual issues of component lifecycles, asynchronous notification, and sharing mutable data across threads, all apply. It would be very nice to have frameworks that helped to hide the complexities and made it easy to do the right thing.

What would such a framework look like? What would the perfect asynchronous scheduling framework do for the developer? The wish list might look something like this:

- The framework should support thread safety.

- The framework should be Android component lifecycle-aware.

- The framework should make smart use of process priority.

- The framework should be power-thrifty.

Let's examine these requirements in some detail.

Thread Safety

An asynchronous scheduling mechanism is likely to involve multiple threads. If it does, all the complexity inherent in concurrent code discussed in the previous chapters applies. A good framework should make it easy to see what code is running on which thread in order to prevent accidentally shared state. It should also provide a mechanism for safe publication for use when state sharing is necessary.

Lifecycle-Aware

A good scheduling framework should interact correctly with the lifecycles of Android components. It should be difficult, using the framework, to leak memory by holding references to components that have been destroyed.

Ideally, it should be possible to schedule an event to occur even when the application that scheduled that event is not running. A scheduled event should restart the app.

Smart Use of Process Priority

A scheduling framework that supports scheduling events at times when the application that scheduled those events is not the application visible on the screen, is not running at all, or possibly even when the phone is in low-power mode, must be prepared to manage process priority and **wake-locks**. If the device is in low power mode, the framework must seize a wake-lock to keep it from returning to low power before the event is completely processed.

Equally important, once the event has been processed, it must release the wake-lock to minimize battery impact.

A good framework must also adjust the priority of the process that powers it (lower the `oom_adj`) to notify Android's process management system that the process is doing useful work and should not be terminated to free memory.

Note

A Wake-lock is a low-level power management facility used by Android to keep a device powered up while it is doing useful work. Android manages power using a feature called "opportunistic suspension." When opportunistic suspension is enabled, the kernel is very aggressive about entering a low-power state. It puts the system to sleep unless there is at least one wake-lock. User-space applications are responsible for seizing and releasing wake-locks as necessary.

Wake-locks were originally hacked into the Android fork of the Linux kernel by the Android development team. After several years of acrimonious debate, the main line Linux kernel now contains a feature called "suspend blockers" that support wake-lock functionality.

When a device is in a low power state, it is clear that no wake-locks exist. If an event occurs when the device is in this state, the event recipient must be sure to seize a wake-lock as quickly as possible or risk having the device go back to sleep before the event is completely processed.

Power-Thrifty

There are many ways to be frugal with power, but one of the most important is by clustering tasks.

Imagine a device whose owner has installed several applications, each of which needs to do twenty or thirty minutes of synchronization daily. The designers of these applications, each doing his or her best to schedule this work at night when the impact on the user is least, chooses a random half-hour period between midnight and 5 AM. As the number of such applications increases, so do the chances that the device spends a substantial portion of the night powered up. The impact on the battery could be reduced dramatically if all applications did their synchronization concurrently, during the same half hour, enabling the device to sleep the rest of the night.

Task clustering becomes even more important when the tasks use the cellular radio. Because powering up the cell radio is typically the second most expensive thing a device can do, clustering network use is an extremely important way to save power.

It is impossible for a user application to have a global view of other applications' scheduled tasks. Clustering tasks is something that can only be done with a system-wide overview.

> **Note**
>
> Cellular radio power management is a complex and interesting subject. Most modern radios have three states, a low-power state, a standby state and an active state. Understanding these states and how they are used can mean the difference between a power-thrifty app and a battery hog. Ilya Grigorik's *High Performance Browser Networking* (O'Reilly, 2013) contains clear and complete discussions of the issue and is a valuable resource for anyone designing connected mobile applications.

The Scorecard

Table 7.1 shows the list of requirements as a scorecard, to be used to evaluate various scheduling techniques. Each framework earns between 0 and 5 points on each of four axes.

Table 7.1   **The Scorecard**

Framework	Thread-safe	Lifecycle-aware	Process priority-aware	Power-thrifty
A framework	0	2	4	5

Let's rate some frameworks!

Timer and TimerTask

Java's `Timer` and `TimerTask` classes are included here only for completeness. Some Android applications still use them, and answers on Stack Overflow still occasionally recommend them. Even in desktop Java, however, they are obsolete if not deprecated. Instead of a `Timer`, modern applications use the executor framework and the `ScheduledThreadPoolExecutor`.

Chapter 2, "Java Concurrency," discussed the reason for avoiding arbitrary thread creation. That discussion applies directly to the `Timer`. An application should have a policy for the number of threads it spawns. Creating new threads for new tasks (as `TimerTask` does) is not a good policy.

The scorecard in Table 7.2 includes the Timer, but does not score it. Do not use `Timer` or `TimerTask` in your applications (Android or otherwise).

Table 7.2   **The Scorecard: Timer Tasks**

Framework	Thread-safe	Lifecycle-aware	Process priority-aware	Power-thrifty
Timer and TimerTask	NA	NA	NA	NA

Looper/Handler

Chapter 5, "Looper/Hander," discussed the Looper/Handler framework in detail. The discussion demonstrated scheduling a task for execution at some future time. Turning this into a framework for periodic scheduling requires only that a task reschedule itself every time it runs. Listing 7.1 is an example of a simple periodic scheduling framework based on Looper/Handler.

Listing 7.1 **Periodic Looper Task**

```
public class PeriodicTaskScheduler {
  private static final int PERIODIC_TASK = -1230;

  public interface Task { void onTask(); }

  public static final class TaskInfo {
    final long interval;
    final Task task;
    volatile boolean cancelled;
    TaskInfo(Task task, long interval) {
      this.task = task;
      this.interval = interval;
    }
  }

  private static class PeriodicTaskHandler extends Handler {
    public PeriodicTaskHandler(Looper looper) { super(looper); }

    @Override
    public void handleMessage(Message msg) {
      if (msg.what != PERIODIC_TASK) { return; }
      long t = SystemClock.elapsedRealtime();

      TaskInfo info = (TaskInfo) msg.obj;
      if (!info.cancelled) {
        info.task.onTask();
        scheduleTask(msg.what, info, t);
      }
    }

    public void scheduleTask(int what, TaskInfo info, long t) {
      Message msg = obtainMessage(what, info);
      sendMessageAtTime(msg, t + info.interval);
    }
  }


  private final PeriodicTaskHandler handler;

  public PeriodicTaskScheduler(Looper looper) {
    handler = new PeriodicTaskHandler(looper);
  }
```

```
public TaskInfo scheduleTask(Task task, long interval) {
  TaskInfo info = new TaskInfo(task, interval);
  handler.scheduleTask(PERIODIC_TASK, info, SystemClock.elapsedRealtime());
  return info;
}

public void stopTask(TaskInfo info) {
  info.cancelled = true;
}
}
```

A scheduling framework like this has a lot to recommend it. It is fairly full-featured. It can use either an existing Looper or one created specifically for the purpose. Tasks can be scheduled and cancelled individually. The code is small and parsimonious with resources. As described in Chapter 5, it will have only minimal impact on garbage collection.

There are some substantial downsides, though. The two most obvious are the same that haunt so many concurrent structures in Android: thread-safety and lifecycle incongruence. The callback to the onEvent method will take place on whatever worker thread is associated with the Looper that is used to initialize the scheduler. The class implementing the Task interface is likely to have to be thread-safe.

Taking a page from the implementation of AsyncTasks, the framework could be extended to enqueue the call to onEvent back on the Looper from which scheduleTask was originally called. It could even enqueue it for a Looper passed as an argument to scheduleTask.

Neither of these changes, however, will alleviate the lifecycle problem. The periodic execution framework holds a reference to the Task that is enqueued for periodic execution until that task is stopped. If the task holds a reference to an Android component either directly or through some other object, it suffers from exactly the same problem that afflicts AsyncTasks, as described in Chapter 4, "AsyncTasks and Loaders."

There are other concerns when using a framework like that in Listing 7.1. Because the Looper/ Handler framework simply sorts a new entry into its task queue according to its scheduled time, a task that actually takes longer to run than the interval at which it is scheduled can starve other tasks on the same queue. Also, note that tasks scheduled in this framework are completely ephemeral; they neither discourage Android from terminating an application, nor survive such termination.

Table 7.3 **The Scorecard: Looper/Handler**

Framework	Thread-safe	Lifecycle-aware	Process priority-aware	Power-thrifty
Timer and TimerTask	NA	NA	NA	NA
Looper/Handler	1	0	0	1

Table 7.3 scores the Looper/Handler framework on the scorecard. The rating is overly pessimistic. Like the AsyncTasks, a Looper/Handler periodic scheduling framework can work very well for certain kinds of tasks. Although completely inappropriate for networking interactions, they are perfect—to choose an obvious example—for updating a display with the current time.

Custom Service-based Scheduler

Many developers end up designing a custom asynchronous execution service. Generally, these services are based on a `ThreadPoolExecutor` and some object representing a task submitted for execution. Such a service could be extended to support scheduled tasks with very little difficulty. Such an extension might use a `ScheduledThreadPoolExecutor` and extend tasks objects to include scheduling information.

The specifics of the design for such a service, though, depend on the exact requirements of the application. The service might, for instance, be extremely simple and require tasks to reschedule themselves (as they did in the Looper/Handler example). On the other hand, the service might support complex scheduling options that enable specifying the type of connectivity, power status, and even geographical location, required to schedule a particular event. Attempting to provide code for all—or even many—of the possible implementations of a custom scheduler is well beyond the scope of this book. The discussion here must be based on generalities.

The general approach, again, has many advantages. A custom schedule can be tailored—or even extended over the lifetime of the application—to have exactly the functionality that the application requires. A well-architected service will adjust process priority so that it is less likely that the application will be interrupted while useful work is being done. It will also makes some effort to isolate thread-safety concerns in a way that makes accidental errors less likely.

Choosing to create and maintain a custom scheduler, however, is a big decision. All the bugs belong to you, the developer, and the implementation improves only when you and your team improve it. In addition, a scheduling service that is part of an application has very limited access to system-level information about power and connectivity. It certainly will never have the system-wide view necessary to do task clustering.

Table 7.4 **The Scorecard: Custom Service-based Scheduler**

Framework	Thread-safe	Lifecycle-aware	Process priority-aware	Power-thrifty
Timer and TimerTask	NA	NA	NA	NA
Looper/Handler	1	0	0	1
Service-based Scheduler	3	2	3	2

Table 7.4 scores the service-based scheduler. It can work quite well. Many of the most common and popular applications use one or more of them. They are a lot of code to own, though. It would be great if there were a better alternative.

Alarm Manager and Intent Service

Chapter 6, "Services, Processes, and IPC," introduced the IntentService, a simple combination of a service and a Looper/Handler that executes tasks, identified by Intents, on a background thread. Combining the IntentService with the AlarmManager creates a very useful framework for scheduling periodic tasks.

The AlarmManager is a system-level service used to schedule the delivery of a *PendingIntent* at some time in the future. It is capable of waking a device that is in a low-power state, and scheduling alarms that are persistent across process boundaries. Listing 7.2 demonstrates the use of the AlarmManager to start and stop the execution of a sample task.

Listing 7.2 **Periodic Scheduling with the AlarmManager**

```java
public class AlarmScheduler extends IntentService {
  private static final String TAG = "SCHEDULER";

  private static final String PARAM_TASK = TAG + ".TASK";
  private static final int SAMPLE_TASK = -1;

  public static void startSampleTask(Context ctxt) {
    int interval
      = ctxt.getResources().getInteger(R.integer.sample_task_interval);
    ((AlarmManager) ctxt.getSystemService(Context.ALARM_SERVICE))
      .setInexactRepeating(
        AlarmManager.ELAPSED_REALTIME,
        SystemClock.elapsedRealtime() + 100,
        TimeUnit.MILLISECONDS.convert(interval, TimeUnit.MINUTES),
        getTaskIntent(ctxt, SAMPLE_TASK));
  }

  public static void stopSampleTask(Context ctxt) {
    ((AlarmManager) ctxt.getSystemService(Context.ALARM_SERVICE))
      .cancel(getTaskIntent(ctxt, SAMPLE_TASK));
  }

  private static PendingIntent getTaskIntent(Context ctxt, int taskId) {
    Intent intent = new Intent(ctxt, AlarmScheduler.class);
    intent.putExtra(PARAM_TASK, taskId);
    return PendingIntent.getService(
      ctxt,
      taskId,
      intent,
      PendingIntent.FLAG_UPDATE_CURRENT);
  }

  // ...
}
```

> **Note**
>
> A `PendingIntent` is a way to enable an external process to perform an operation as if it were the process that originally created the operation.
>
> One way to think about PendingIntents is as notes to a future self. An application can put instructions into a PendingIntent envelope and then hand the envelope to some other application. At some point, the other application puts the envelope into the mail. The original application receives the envelope, opens it, and follows its own previously written instructions.

In Listing 7.2, the static method `startSampleTask` obtains a reference to the `AlarmManager` and uses it to schedule a `PendingIntent` for periodic delivery by calling the method `setInexactRepeating`. The first argument to `setInexactRepeating` is the scheduling mode. The second and third arguments control the time of the first delivery of the PendingIntent and the repetition interval after that. All these parameters will be discussed in detail shortly.

The static method `stopSampleTask` cancels the periodic task. It creates a PendingIntent by using the same method that `startSampleTask` did: `getTaskIntent`. It then calls the `AlarmManager` method `cancel`. Using the same method to generate the PendingIntent for both the start and stop methods guarantees that they are identical. In particular, the integer tag that is the second argument to the `getService` method in `getTaskIntent` is identical for both methods. PendingIntents with different tags cannot be identical.

The flag that is the fourth argument to `getService`, `FLAG_UPDATE_CURRENT`, enables the PendingIntent to be refreshed and delivered multiple times. There are several other flags. Do not use `ONE_SHOT` for repeating tasks!

The actual Intent that will drive the execution of the sample task is the one created in the first couple of lines of `getTaskIntent`. It is an explicit Intent that will be delivered to `AlarmScheduler`'s `onHandleIntent` method. As in the Looper/Handler, an opcode—the value stored in the Intent extras with the key `PARAM_TASK`—will identify the specific task to be executed, `SAMPLE_TASK`.

The Alarm Manager Service

It is the `AlarmManagerService`, a system service, that will actually deliver the scheduled PendingIntent. The `AlarmManagerService` is a component in a separate application that interfaces with hardware to enable it to wake up and deliver events even when the device is in a low-power state. The Android system runs it at startup and it stays running until the device is powered down. It is always running. That is something that no user application can do. Because of this, it can restart an application that has been stopped, to deliver a scheduled Intent to it.

The `AlarmManager` API is a thin wrapper around an inter-process communication connection to the `AlarmManagerService`. Calls to the local `AlarmManager` are sent, nearly unaltered, to the `AlarmManagerService`.

The `AlarmManagerService` will refuse to schedule an event in the past. Because the call to `setInexactRepeating` is actually IPC, it can take a significant amount of time. Attempting to schedule an event at the current time can occasionally fail because by the time the service processes the message, the formerly current time is now in the past. It is good practice to schedule the first event at least a little bit in the future: 100ms is easily enough.

The scheduling modes supported by the `AlarmManagerService` can be confusing. This is particularly true because the way in which those modes are applied has changed over the course of Android's evolution. Ignoring one-off tasks—tasks scheduled for a single execution—there are three dimensions in task scheduling: clock type, scheduling window size, and power regimen.

Clock type is simplest of the dimensions. There are two kinds of clocks, wall-clock, `RTC`, and elapsed-time clock, `ELAPSED_REALTIME`. The former uses `System.currentTimeMillis` and the latter `SystemClock.elapsedRealtime`. Both clocks count the time during which a device is asleep. They differ, though, in that wall-clock time can go backward (set by the user or the phone network) and elapsed time cannot. Use `RTC` to schedule an event at 18:00 every day. Use `ELAPSED_REALTIME` to schedule an event at 24-hour intervals.

Consistency is essential! When using an `ELAPSED_REALTIME` mode, for instance, be sure to schedule the first delivery using `SystemClock.elapsedRealtime`. Confusing the two clock types will result in the first delivery being scheduled far, far in the future or not at all.

Related to the clock type is the scheduling window size. Task batching, especially for tasks that might use the radio, is one of the goals in the scorecard. The `AlarmManagerService` definitely supports task batching, but that support has changed over releases.

Prior to API level 19 (KitKat), the two methods `setInexactRepeating` and `setRepeating` scheduled tasks that would and would not be batched, respectively. Tasks scheduled inexactly could be moved up to 75% of their scheduled interval, to group them with other tasks. This is still true for an application that targets API level 18 or earlier.

For apps targeting API level 19 or later, however, the two methods are identical: both schedule tasks inexactly. There is no simple way for a recent app to schedule a repeating task exactly. The only way to do it is to schedule a one-time task that reschedules itself when it runs, as it did in the Looper/Handler framework.

The `AlarmManagerService`, with its use of IPC, PendingIntents and a hardware interface, is a very heavyweight mechanism to use for scheduling frequent tasks. The overhead, combined with the time variation introduced by batching, makes scheduling tasks with repeat intervals in single-digit minutes unwise. Recent versions of Android have even made it impossible to schedule tasks at intervals smaller than a minute altogether.

Although the `AlarmManagerService` is capable of rousing a device from low-power states, the code in Listing 7.2 will not do so because it is not using one of the `_WAKEUP` scheduling modes. In non-wakeup modes, the `AlarmManagerService` adds the key `Intent.EXTRA_ALARM_COUNT` to the Bundle extras of the Intent it delivers to the target application. The value associated with that key is an integer giving the number of events that were not delivered because the device was asleep at the time at which the event was scheduled.

Using one of the _WAKEUP scheduling modes is an expensive thing to do to the battery and is not a decision to be made lightly. It also requires some changes to the code. Unless someone seizes a wake-lock, the kernel's opportunistic suspension mechanism will force the device back into the low-power state immediately. The AlarmManagerService holds a wake-lock while it is processing alarms. It releases the wake-lock, though, once it delivers the PendingIntent. Oddly, the meaning of "delivers" depends on whether the target for the PendingIntent is a BroadcastReceiver or a Service. All PendingIntents are not created equal.

In Listing 7.2, the PendingIntent is created using a call to getService. When the AlarmManagerService delivers such a PendingIntent, it releases the wake-lock *before* the target application acknowledges receiving the Intent. It is impossible under these conditions to guarantee that there is no wake-lock gap; the AlarmManagerService can release its wake-lock before the target application seizes its.

Fortunately, PendingIntents created with the method getBroadcast are handled differently. The AlarmManagerService does not release its wake-lock until the target application's onReceive method returns. Seizing a wake-lock in the onReceive method guarantees that there is no gap. To use either of the _WAKEUP scheduling modes safely, the PendingIntent must be delivered to a BroadcastReceiver that seizes a wake-lock in its onReceive method. The Android v4 Support Library provides exactly such a BroadcastReceiver, the WakefulBroadcastReceiver. Listing 7.3 demonstrates the changes necessary to receive events that awaken the system safely.

Listing 7.3 **Low-power Periodic Scheduling with the Alarm Manager**

```
// ...

public static class AlarmReceiver extends WakefulBroadcastReceiver {
  @Override
  public void onReceive(Context ctxt, Intent intent) {
    Intent svcIntent = new Intent(ctxt, AlarmScheduler.class);
    svcIntent.putExtras(intent);
    startWakefulService(ctxt, svcIntent);
  }
}

public static void startSampleTask(Context ctxt) {
  int interval = ctxt.getResources().getInteger(R.integer.sample_task_interval);
  ((AlarmManager) ctxt.getSystemService(Context.ALARM_SERVICE))
    .setInexactRepeating(
      AlarmManager.ELAPSED_REALTIME_WAKEUP,  //!!! Wakeup!
      SystemClock.elapsedRealtime() + 100,
      TimeUnit.MILLISECONDS.convert(interval, TimeUnit.MINUTES),
      getTaskIntent(ctxt, SAMPLE_TASK));
}

// ...
```

```
private static PendingIntent getTaskIntent(Context ctxt, int taskId) {
  Intent intent = new Intent(ctxt, AlarmReceiver.class); // target receiver
  intent.putExtra(PARAM_TASK, taskId);
  return PendingIntent.getBroadcast( // target receiver
    ctxt,
    taskId,
    intent,
    PendingIntent.FLAG_UPDATE_CURRENT);
}
// ...
```

The most significant change in Listing 7.3 is the addition of the `AlarmReceiver` class. It does nothing other than forward the extras from any Intent it receives to the AlarmScheduler service after seizing a wake-lock.

The `AlarmReceiver` is a `WakefulBroadcastReceiver` and is registered in the application manifest, as shown in Listing 7.4.

Listing 7.4 Manifest for Low-power Scheduler

```
<manifest
  xmlns:android="http://schemas.android.com/apk/res/android"
  package="net.callmeike.android.intentservicescheduler"
  >

  <uses-permission android:name="android.permission.WAKE_LOCK"/>

  <application
    android:allowBackup="false"
    android:icon="@mipmap/ic_launcher"
    android:label="@string/app_name"
    android:supportsRtl="true"
    android:theme="@style/AppTheme"
    >

    <!-- ... -->

    <service android:name=".svc.AlarmScheduler"/>
    <receiver android:name=".svc.AlarmScheduler$AlarmReceiver" />
  </application>

</manifest>
```

Listing 7.4 also highlights another important detail. Seizing wake-locks is a potentially dangerous capability and as such requires permission. To use the `WakefulBroadcastReceiver`, an application must request `WAKE_LOCK` permission.

There are three other smaller changes in Listing 7.3. First, the Intent constructed at the top of `getTaskIntent` targets the receiver, not the service. Next, the PendingIntent that wraps it is a broadcast Intent (`getBroadcast`), not a service Intent (`getService`). Finally, the call to `setInexactRepeating` sets wakeup scheduling mode with the flag `ELAPSED_REALTIME_WAKEUP`.

It is worth noting that this implementation is not completely bullet-proof. There is no entirely safe way for an application to release a wake-lock. Given Android's process model, it is impossible to be certain that the code that releases a wake-lock will ever be executed, `finally` block or otherwise. The only safe thing to do is to seize the lock for a constrained time period, using `acquire(long timeout)`, and then to re-acquire it as necessary.

Schedulable Tasks

Recall from Chapter 6 that tasks executed by an IntentService are typically bound fairly tightly to the service that executes them. Unlike some of the other schedulers that have been discussed here, tasks for an IntentService are not usually represented as closures or observers passed into the service. Instead, they are frequently methods in the code of the execution service itself. Adding a new task for execution usually means coding up the task and explicitly calling it from the service.

This constraint is quite apparent in Listings 7.2 and 7.3. All the parameters—the time of the first scheduled event, the interval at which subsequent events occur, all of it—is hidden in the call to scheduling methods. Creating a new schedulable task would require two new methods, for example, `scheduleAnotherTask` and `cancelAnotherTask`, respectively, in addition to the code for the task itself. It is certainly possible to relax these constraints programmatically. It is not so easy to relax them safely.

The first thing to note is that a given PendingIntent can only be scheduled once. Before scheduling a PendingIntent, the `AlarmManagerService` cancels any schedules for any PendingIntents that are `equals`. An attempt to schedule an `equals` PendingIntent a second time will simply replace the previous schedule for that intent.

It might seem obvious that the solution to this would be to create new PendingIntents for each new schedule. And why stop there? Dynamically created PendingIntents could be used to represent arbitrary tasks, passed to a generic scheduler. We could throw off the oppressive straightjacket of tight task binding present in Listings 7.2 and 7.3! Free periodic scheduling for everyone!

Sadly, Android's component lifecycle model rules with an iron hand. For a dynamically created PendingIntent strategy to work, the meaning of a scheduled intent would have to be stored in a way that was persistent across process boundaries.

Consider a scheduler similar to the service in Listing 7.2 that dynamically creates a new pending Intent for a new task given to it for scheduling. It creates a new, unique ID and uses that ID both as `PARAM_TASK` and as the tag for the PendingIntent. It also uses the ID to store a reference to the task to be run in a `SparseArray`. When the Intent is delivered, it looks up the task in the array and runs it. Life is good.

Eventually, though, the application is killed. All applications are. Suppose that thirty-seven minutes after it is killed the `AlarmManagerService` wakes the device from a deep sleep, restarts the application, and faithfully delivers that PendingIntent. Sadly, there is nothing in the scheduler's array of tasks! It has forgotten what it was supposed to do!

Making schedulable tasks persistent is hard enough to do that it is simply an unreasonable effort for most applications. On the other hand, some isolation, especially isolation that would enable the task to be tested independently of the scheduling framework seems like a very good idea. Listing 7.5 shows the `onHandleIntent` method of the AlarmScheduler as it might look using a dependency injection framework—in this case, Dagger 2. An architecture like this separates the tasks from the Service that runs them. This makes testing task code dramatically easier.

Listing 7.5   **Alarm Scheduler Task Execution**

```
public class AlarmScheduler extends IntentService {

  // ...

  @Inject volatile Lazy<SampleTask> sampleTask;

  public AlarmScheduler() { super(TAG); }

  @Override
  public void onCreate() {
    super.onCreate();
    DaggerTaskComponent.create().inject(this);
  }

  @Override
  protected void onHandleIntent(Intent intent) {
    try {
      int op = intent.getIntExtra(PARAM_TASK, 0);
      switch (op) {
        case SAMPLE_TASK:
          sampleTask.get().run();
          break;
        default:
          Log.w(TAG, "unexpected op: " + op);
      }
    }
    finally {
      AlarmReceiver.completeWakefulIntent(intent);
    }
  }
}
```

> **Note**
>
> Dependency injection frameworks, though outside the scope of this book, are an essential tool for Android developers. They are at this point quite mature, and there are several available, each with its own advantages and disadvantages. They are an extremely effective way of achieving unit testable Android code. Every Android developer should be using at least one.

The dependency injection framework populates the volatile variable `sampleTask` during the call to `DaggerTaskComponent.create().inject()` in the service's `onCreate` method. The variable must be volatile because it is initialized from the UI, but then used from the worker thread.

So, what about the scorecard for the AlarmManager/IntentService based scheduler? It has all the advantages and disadvantage of an IntentService, discussed in Chapter 6. Its isolation from its client makes it great for thread and lifecycle safety. That same isolation can be frustrating when the scheduled task needs to change a value in a visible view.

All the tasks executed by an IntentService are executed on a single worker thread and in order. That means no surprises, but also that a long-running task can force subsequent tasks off their schedule. An IntentService is perfectly process priority-aware. It starts itself while executing tasks and stops itself when the last task completes.

Used properly, the AlarmManager does provide some wake-lock management. Best of all, because it has a system-wide purview, it can cluster tasks. This is a very significant advantage. It is the first scheduling mechanism discussed so far that can do this.

On the down side, AlarmManager schedules, although persistent across processes, are not persistent across reboot. If necessary, an application must catch the `BOOT_COMPLETE` broadcast to reschedule its alarms at system start.

Also, nothing in this framework supports scheduling tasks depending on radio, power, or network state. Athough it is possible to determine some of those things using other APIs, there is no built-in support.

Table 7.5   **The Scorecard: Custom, Service-based Scheduler**

Framework	Thread-safe	Lifecycle-aware	Process priority-aware	Power-thrifty
Timer and TimerTask	NA	NA	NA	NA
Looper/Handler	1	0	0	1
Service-based Scheduler	3	2	3	2
AlarmManager/ IntentService	4	4	4	3

Table 7.5 gives the score—not bad. Although this framework can work very well for some requirements, it is still not a panacea. There is plenty of room for improvement.

Sync-Adapters

The discussion in this chapter so far has been about implementation: how to execute a task on a periodic schedule. Perhaps we need to take a step back. Perhaps, instead of looking at ways of scheduling tasks periodically, we should consider why periodic tasks are needed in the first place. We need to move abstraction up a level.

The so-called sync-adapter is one such higher-level abstraction. At its essence, it is a connection between a local dataset, identified by a "content" URL, and an external, credentialed account.

The canonical example of a synchronized dataset that might be managed by a sync-adapter is a contacts list. All of a user's devices have an identical view of the user's contacts because they all synchronize with a central datastore. The central datastore is protected by authentication, so that only the owning user has access to the list of contacts.

Sync-adapters have been around for a long time: at least since Éclair (API Level 5). In the early days of the platform they were very poorly documented, and getting the configuration even slightly wrong could crash the entire operating system. Recently, though, they seem to have gotten much more stable, and the documentation has improved dramatically (though to this day an incorrectly implemented account can crash the system Settings application). Adding a sync-adapter to an application is now a fairly straightforward and common practice.

Sync-adapters are complex beasts, and a complete tutorial for creating them is out of scope for this discussion. The goal here is to understand how they work well enough to rate them accurately against the scorecard.

Creating a sync-adapter is a multistep process.

- Define the sync-adapter linking a ContentProvider authority and account type.

- Define the account type.

- Define the ContentProvider.

- Define the AccountAuthenticator Service.

- Define the SyncAdapter Service.

- Implement the SyncAdapterService and the SyncAdapter.

- Implement the ContentProvider.

- Implement the AccountAuthenticatorService and AccountAuthenticator.

The last two steps, actual implementation of the ContentProvider and AccountAuthenticator, are the topics that are entirely outside the scope of a discussion of periodic task management. A web search for either topic will turn up a wide variety of resources.

> **Note**
>
> The ContentProvider is among the most powerful and interesting abstractions in Android. A ContentProvider presents a RESTful API for a local dataset in a way that that blurs the distinction between local and remote data. With a bit of mind-bending magic, they also enable a URI to represent the data available through it, supporting a particularly elegant Model-View-Controller-like architecture.
>
> "Enterprise Android," Mednieks, Dornin, Meike, Pan discusses this architecture in detail.

Defining a Sync-adapter

The first step in creating a sync-adapter is writing the special XML resource that defines it. The resource defines the connection between a local dataset and a remote account. Listing 7.6 is an example of a fairly typical sync-adapter definition.

Listing 7.6   **Sync-adapter Definition**

```
<?xml version="1.0" encoding="utf-8"?>
<sync-adapter
  xmlns:android="http://schemas.android.com/apk/res/android"
  android:accountType="@string/account_type"
  android:contentAuthority="net.callmeike.android.simplesync"
  android:userVisible="false"
  android:supportsUploading="true"
  android:allowParallelSyncs="false"
  android:isAlwaysSyncable="true" />
```

The first two attributes, `android:accountType` and `android:contentAuthority` are the important part. They establish the relationship between a group of accounts and a local dataset.

The content authority is the namespace for which some local ContentProvider claims jurisdiction. It represents the dataset.

The account type is analogous to a content authority. It works in a similar way. It is a string for which some local service claims to be the authenticator. Just as any requests for data that use a URI that begins with the content provider's authority will be directed by the system to the sole ContentProvider that owns that authority, so any attempt to use an account whose type is claimed by a particular Service will be directed by the system to that Service for authentication.

Creating, managing, and authenticating accounts is by far the most complex part of creating a sync-adapter. Because a sync-adapter is a link between a content provider and an account type, an account type is necessary for every sync-adapter.

Accounts, though, are not the focus of the current discussion. The account used in this example will be extremely simple. The sample application itself will claim authority for the account type, and will create a single account of the type. The account will require no authentication and will not be visible (as most accounts are) from the Settings application's Accounts page. This example sync-adapter will synchronize local data with an uncredentialed remote.

An account type, like the sync-adapter, is defined in a special XML file. Listing 7.6 is a minimal account type definition.

Listing 7.6   **Account Type Definition**

```
<?xml version="1.0" encoding="utf-8"?>
<account-authenticator
  xmlns:android="http://schemas.android.com/apk/res/android"
  android:accountType="@string/account_type" />
```

The next step is defining the ContentProvider that is the authority for the dataset linked to the account type. ContentProviders are defined in the application manifest, as Listing 7.7 demonstrates.

Listing 7.7   **Content Provider Definition**

```
<?xml version="1.0" encoding="utf-8"?>
<manifest
  xmlns:android="http://schemas.android.com/apk/res/android"
  package="net.callmeike.android.simplesync" >

  <!-- ... -->

  <application
    android:name=".SyncApp"
    android:allowBackup="true"
    android:icon="@drawable/ic_launcher"
    android:label="@string/app_name"
    android:theme="@style/AppTheme" >

    <!-- ... -->

    <provider
      android:name=".data.SyncProvider"
      android:authorities="net.callmeike.android.simplesync"
      android:exported="false" />
  </application>

</manifest>
```

Notice that, perhaps surprisingly, the provider, defined in Listing 7.7, is explicitly not exported (android:exported=false). This means that access to the content provider is protected by the Android system. Most external applications cannot get access to it. There is only one category of applications other than SimpleSync itself that has access to the SyncProvider: system applications. If the system is not trustworthy, there are bigger problems.

> **Note**
>
> Unfortunately, the argument to the provider attribute `android:authorities` cannot be a reference. This is mildly annoying because it means that the name of the authority must be defined in several places and that those definitions must match. Caveat coder.

The sync-adapter is now almost completely defined. Listing 7.5 shows the linking of the account type to the ContentProvider, Listing 7.6 shows the definition of the account type, and Listing 7.7 shows the definition of the ContentProvider.

The last step in defining the sync-adapter is to make it visible in the manifest. For reasons that will become obvious in a moment, this is done inside the declaration of a Service. Listing 7.8 shows the Service declaration.

Listing 7.8 **The Sync-adapter Service**

```
<service
    android:name=".SyncService"
    android:exported="false">

    <!-- ... -->

    <meta-data
        android:name="android.content.SyncAdapter"
        android:resource="@xml/sync"/>
</service>
```

When the SimpleSync application is installed on a device, the Android system parses the manifest. When decoding the declaration of its Service, it finds the metadata with the special name of `android.content.SyncAdapter` and recognizes the resource named in its `android:resource` attribute as the definition of a sync-adapter. It records the definition in a system-level database of sync-adapters and completes the installation.

How Sync-adapters Work

Before continuing with a discussion of the implementation of a sync-adapter, it will be enlightening to explore how they work.

Leaping ahead, suppose that the application SimpleSync now contains a fully-implemented sync-adapter, has been installed on an Android device, and that it is time for the sync-adapter to run. Figure 7.1 illustrates the process by which the Android system invokes its sync-adapter.

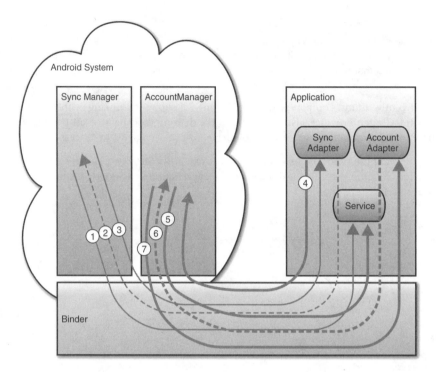

Figure 7.1   Running a sync-adapter

The process begins (Figure 7.1, arrow #1) when the Android SyncManager service determines that a sync-adapter needs to be run. The SyncManager is (as was the AlarmManager) a component of a system application, the ContentService. It is a separate process, running in its own process space. Just as the AlarmManager did, it uses Binder to establish an inter-process connection to the application that is associated with the particular sync-adapter. As usual, this can have the side effect of restarting the target application if it is not already running to set up the IPC connection.

Chapter 6 described the connection process. Recall that to make the connection to the target application, the ContentService looks for a Service that has an intent filter for the action `android.content.SyncAdapter`. The SimpleSync application has such a service. That Service is the factory that creates the sync-adapter object and returns the IPC connection to it, to the SyncManager (Figure 7.1, arrow #2). The SyncManager can now make IPC calls to the sync-adapter running in the target application.

Because an account type was associated with the sync-adapter in its declaration in the manifest, the SyncManager already knows which account to use, as it prepares to make the call that will start the sync-adapter. When it makes the call (Figure 7.1, arrow #3), it passes that account to the sync-adapter.

Remember that a sync-adapter is a connection between an account and a dataset. The SyncManager will only run a sync-adapter for an existing account. If there is no account of the type associated with the sync-adapter, the SyncManager will never run. To schedule periodic runs of a sync-adapter, at least one account of the account type associated with the sync-adapter must exist.

When a typical sync-adapter starts, it will usually validate the account that was passed to it. It does so with an IPC process that is nearly the reverse of that by which the SyncManager connected to SimpleSync. Instead of the system service connecting to the target application, this time the target application makes an IPC call to the AccountManager (Figure 7.1, arrow #4). There are now two IPC connections open. That is by no means the end of it, either.

Because the target application has declared in its manifest that it is responsible for authenticating accounts of the type for which authentication was just requested, the AccountManager creates yet another IPC connection, the third, back to the target app! Again, it does this by finding the application that is registered as the owner of the account type, and finding within it a Service that has an intent filter for the particular action `android.accounts.AccountAuthenticator` (Figure 7.1, arrow #5). This could be any application at all. In this example, however, as will often be the case, the application that defines the sync-adapter is also the application that manages the account type. The Service is a factory for an account manager and the IPC connection to it (Figure 7.1, arrow #6).

The AccountManager service now requests, over the IPC connection, that the account authenticator authenticate the account (Figure 7.1, arrow #7). The authenticator has complete control over the process. In the simplest case, the account was already validated at some time in the past and requires at most refreshing an OAuth token. The process can be nearly arbitrarily complex, though. It might require logging in to a remote web site, reading a fingerprint sensor, or casting runes.

Eventually, at least in the happy case, the authenticator authenticates the account and tells the account manager that all is well. The account manager tells the sync-adapter that the account is good and the sync-adapter runs, synchronizing data between the authenticated account and the content provider.

Implementing the Sync-adapter

It is straightforward to infer, from the previous description, the additions needed in the SimpleSync service definition. The SimpleSync application needs services that act as factories for the sync-adapter itself, and for the account authenticator for the sync-adapter's associated account type. A single service can actually do both. Listing 7.9 shows, in its entirety, the definition of the Service, started in Listing 7.8.

Listing 7.9   **Complete Sync-adapter Service**

```
<service
  android:name=".SyncService"
  android:exported="false">
  <intent-filter>
    <action android:name="android.accounts.AccountAuthenticator"/>
    <action android:name="android.content.SyncAdapter"/>
  </intent-filter>

  <meta-data
    android:name="android.accounts.AccountAuthenticator"
    android:resource="@xml/account"/>

  <meta-data
    android:name="android.content.SyncAdapter"
    android:resource="@xml/sync"/>
</service>
```

In addition to exposing the sync-adapter metadata definition, the service now exposes an account authenticator metadata definition and links it to the account type whose definition appeared in Listing 7.6. It also defines an intent filter that enables both the SyncManager and the AccountManager to find the service for their respective IPC connections.

As noted in the description of the sync-adapter process, the Service is simply a factory for the sync-adapter and the account authenticator. It is not the implementation of either. There is no reason at all that a single service cannot be the factory for both. SyncService, the implementation of the service defined in Listing 7.9, will do exactly that. Listing 7.10 shows it.

Listing 7.10   **Sync-adapter Service Implementation**

```
public class SyncService extends Service {
  private static final String ACTION_BIND_SYNC = "android.content.SyncAdapter";

  private SyncAdapter syncAdapter;

  @Override
  public void onCreate() {
    super.onCreate();
    syncAdapter = new SyncAdapter(getApplication(), true);
  }

  @Override
  public IBinder onBind(Intent intent) {
    switch (intent.getAction()) {
      case ACTION_BIND_SYNC:
        return syncAdapter.getSyncAdapterBinder();
```

```
      default:
        return null;
    }
  }
}
```

The code in Listing 7.10 creates a singleton instance of the SyncAdapter and returns it to any call to onBind for which the Intent action is android.content.SyncAdapter. As noted before, this is the Intent that the SyncManager uses to connect to the SyncAdapter.

The big shortcut here is that the Service returns a null for every other request. This will include the request from the AccountManager for an account authenticator. SimpleSync does not have an account authenticator and will never be able to validate an account. If, however, the sync-adapter never requests account authentication, this will work just fine.

Note that even though the service returns null in response to a request for an authenticator, the account type must be defined, attached to a service, and that service must have an intent filter for the action android.content.SyncAdapter. Unless all these conditions are met, the Android framework will not run the sync-adapter.

Once this boilerplate is in place, all that is left is to implement the sync-adapter. Listing 7.11 is the adapter from the SimpleSync application.

Listing 7.11   **Sync-adapter Implementation**

```
public class SyncAdapter extends AbstractThreadedSyncAdapter {
  private static final String TAG = "SYNC";

  public SyncAdapter(Context ctxt, boolean autoInitialize) {
    super(ctxt, autoInitialize);
  }

  @Override
  public void onPerformSync(
    Account account,
    Bundle extras,
    String authority,
    ContentProviderClient provider,
    SyncResult result)
  {
    SyncStats stats = result.stats;

    String url = AccountManager.get(getContext())
      .getUserData(account, SyncApp.KEY_URI);
    if (null == url) {
      Log.w(TAG, "Account has no uri: " + account);
      stats.numAuthExceptions++;
```

```
      return;
    }

    Context ctxt = getContext();
    Intent intent = new Intent(ctxt, SyncService.class);

    ctxt.startService(intent);
    try { stats.numInserts += new SimpleSync().sync(url, provider); }
    catch (RemoteException e) {
      Log.e(TAG, "sync failed: " + e);
      stats.numParseExceptions++;
    }
    catch (IOException e) {
      Log.e(TAG, "sync failed: " + e);
      stats.numIoExceptions++;
    }
    finally { ctxt.stopService(intent); }
  }
}
```

Listing 7.11 is the implementation of the sync-adapter created by the SyncService (Listing 7.9) and to which the system SyncManager connects via IPC. The sync-adapter must subclass AbstractThreadedSyncAdapter, and must implement the method onPerformSync, which is called to start the adapter.

Commonly, a sync-adapter would call the AccountManager method blockingGetAuthToken early on to authenticate the account passed to it. In this drastically simplified version, however, the code simply checks to see that there is an endpoint URI associated with the account and treats its absence as an authentication error.

So where did the account come from? That is one more bit of code, shown in Listing 7.12.

Listing 7.12 **Simple Account Creation**

```
public class SyncApp extends Application {
  private static final String TAG = "APP";
  public static final String CANONICAL_ACCOUNT = "SimpleSync";
  public static final String KEY_URI = "SyncAdapter.URI";


  private AccountManager mgr;
  private String acctType;

  @Override
  public void onCreate() {
    super.onCreate();
    Log.d(TAG, "up");
```

```
    mgr = AccountManager.get(this);
    acctType = getString(R.string.account_type);

    if (getAccount() == null) { createAccount(); }
}

public Account getAccount() {
  Account[] accounts = mgr.getAccountsByType(acctType);
  int accountNum = accounts.length;
  if (accountNum > 1) { Log.w(TAG, "Unexpected accounts: " + accountNum); }
  return (accountNum < 1) ? null : accounts[0];
}

private void createAccount() {
  Account account = new Account(CANONICAL_ACCOUNT, acctType);

  mgr.addAccountExplicitly(account, null, null);
  mgr.setUserData(account, KEY_URI, getString(R.string.server_uri));

  ContentResolver.setIsSyncable(account, SyncContract.AUTHORITY, 1);
  ContentResolver.setSyncAutomatically(account, SyncContract.AUTHORITY, true);
  ContentResolver.addPeriodicSync(
    account,
    SyncContract.AUTHORITY,
    new Bundle(),
    getResources().getInteger(R.integer.sync_interval_secs));

  Log.d(TAG, "create account: " + account);
  }
}
```

The code in Listing 7.12 is taken from the SyncApp class. Listing 7.7 shows it registered as the Application object for SimpleSync. The code in the onCreate method ensures that if the application is ever run, one account of the correct account type exists.

The important method in Listing 7.12 is the createAccount method. It does three essential things.

First of all, right at the top, it creates the account. The name associated with the account is hard-coded as CANONICAL_ACCOUNT. An application that supported real accounts would probably get the name from user input.

Next, the code stores the remote's URI as user data associated with the account. In this case, the URI is obtained from an application resource. It is associated with the key KEY_URI, the same key the sync-adapter used to recover it in Listing 7.11. Although this example is very simple, an application could associate an arbitrarily complex URI, containing account names, authentication tokens, and anything else necessary, in the user data for the account.

Finally, using three ContentResolver methods, the code makes this a periodic task. It will be run at the interval specified in the integer resource `R.integer.sync_interval_secs`.

There is one more small detail. Meddling with accounts is, as one might expect, a privileged action. For `SyncApp.createAccount` to work, it needs the three permissions shown in Listing 7.13.

Listing 7.13 **Content Provider Definition**

```xml
<?xml version="1.0" encoding="utf-8"?>
<manifest
  xmlns:android="http://schemas.android.com/apk/res/android"
  package="net.callmeike.android.simplesync" >

  <uses-permission
    android:name="android.permission.GET_ACCOUNTS"/>
  <uses-permission
    android:name="android.permission.AUTHENTICATE_ACCOUNTS"/>
  <uses-permission
    android:name="android.permission.WRITE_SYNC_SETTINGS"/>

  <!-- ... -->

</manifest>
```

Scoring the Sync-adapter

Building a sync-adapter is a lot of work. It requires a Service and ContentProvider, just for openers. It can also require an account authenticator, a complex and tricky project by any standards. Is it worth the trouble?

Sync adapters have some very important advantages. Both sync-adapter and AlarmService base tasks are driven by an interprocess communication connection from a long-lived system application. They are run when they are scheduled to run, whether the application of which they are a component is already running or not. If the sync-adapter's application is not already running when the sync-adapter is scheduled, the system starts the application as a side effect. Sync-adapter schedules survive process boundaries.

Better yet (and unlike AlarmService-based schedules, which must be reinstalled after a device is powered off), sync-adapter schedules *do* survive a reboot. A sync-adapter resumes normal periodic execution when the device is powered back up, without any further action on the part of the scheduling application. That alone is enough to make them the scheduling system of choice, for many applications.

Furthermore, the Android system holds a wake-lock on behalf of the sync-adapter for the entire time that it is running. The sync-adapter is guaranteed that the system will not power down while it is processing and that the system will correctly release the wake-lock held on its behalf, even if it terminates abnormally.

Sync-adapters run in a fairly component-safe environment. They correctly separate front-end, UI processing from the back-end work of synchronizing remote data with a local cache of that data. The lifecycles of the objects required by a sync-adapter are likely to be congruent with the lifecycle of the adapter itself. The normal caveats about storing references to ephemeral data into static variables certainly apply. The sync-adapter environment, however, is relatively "gottcha-free."

Unfortunately, although sync-adapters automatically support power management, they do not automatically support process management. A sync-adapter is a bound, not a started, service and therefore runs with no special enhancement to its priority. To raise the priority of the sync-adapter, it must start (and, of course, stop) a service.

A service that is both bound and started is called a hybrid service. Listing 7.11 demonstrates a hybrid sync-adapter by starting the same service that is bound by the SyncManager. That single overworked service is now serving three distinct roles:

- It is the factory from which the SyncManager obtains an IPC connection to the SyncAdapter.

- It is the factory from which the AccountManager obtains the IPC connection to the AccountAuthenticator. SimpleSync does no account authentication and always returns a null authenticator.

- It is the service started by the sync-adapter that informs the Android system that there is important background work taking place, and that the containing process should get special consideration.

There are several ways of scheduling a sync-adapter. The most familiar is to run it, as you would an AlarmService task, at a specified interval, as demonstrated in Listing 7.12. Just as with the AlarmService-based tasks, sync-adapter runs are scheduled by a system application with a global perspective. They are batched globally across applications and with similar power savings for both radio and battery.

A second way of running a sync-adapter, though, is to schedule it to run when the device already has an open TCP/IP connection. If the device already has a connection open, then the sync-adapter is piggybacking on a radio that is already in use. Because the radio is the most expensive programmatically controlled use of battery power, this method of scheduling a sync-adapter is extremely attractive.

A sync-adapter can also be scheduled explicitly. A very common use of this capability is scheduling the adapter in response to an incoming push notification (for example, Google Cloud Messaging, or an equivalent). When used in this manner, the remote server notifies the application that it should update itself using the push notification, and the application runs the sync-adapter to pull the updates. The application becomes a component in the MVC pattern. It behaves exactly as a View, for a remote Model.

Finally, exactly as one might predict given the MVC pattern, a sync-adapter can also act as a Controller, pushing local updates to the remote when they occur. This behavior is accomplished with one of the cutest tricks in all Android.

The standard way of notifying observers that data represented by a ContentProvider URI has changed is by using the `ContentResolver` method `notifyChange`. In its most common use, this method takes two arguments: the URI representing the data that has changed, and a reference to the observer that initiated the change. Listing 7.14 shows a typical example.

Listing 7.14 **Dataset Change Notification**

```
public Uri insert(@NonNull Uri uri, ContentValues vals) {
  long pk = getDb().insert(TABLE, NULLABLE_COL, vals);

  if (0 > pk) { return null; }

  uri = uri.buildUpon().appendPath(String.valueOf(pk)).build();
  getContext().getContentResolver().notifyChange(uri, null);

  return uri;
}
```

The `insert` method inserts a row into the database corresponding to the passed URI and then notifies all registered listeners that the dataset has changed. The registered listeners will receive a callback and can take appropriate action. A CursorLoader, for instance, like the one discussed in Chapter 4, "AsyncTasks and Loader," might be a view of the dataset the URI represents. It would receive the notification and re-query.

In addition to notifying all listeners, `ContentResolver.notifyChange` also initiates a run of the sync-adapter that is associated with the URI's authority. For example, if called as part of the SimpleSync app, with a URI whose authority component is `net.callmeike.android`
`.simplesync`, the code in Listing 7.14 would cause the app's sync-adapter to run after a short delay. Simply notifying of the change in the usual way causes the associated sync-adapter to synchronize its changes to the remote. Used in this way, sync-adapters implement the complete MVC pattern.

There are two remaining issues. The first is that, when run in this way, the sync-adapter will synchronize *all* the accounts of the type associated with it. In the tiny, single-account SimpleSync application, this is not a problem. In a more complex application, however, that supported multiple accounts, the login process would have to designate the current account and would also have to register an explicit ContentObserver, listening for notifications on the content URI. The Observer would force a sync-adapter run, passing the logged-in account.

The second issue is that an inbound change such as the sync-adapter responding to a push notification will surely cause changes in the database. As coded in Listing 7.14 these inbound changes will trigger an outbound sync. That is not good!

The solution is simple. The two-argument version of `ContentResolver.notifyChange` is a convenience overloading. The full method actually takes three arguments. The third argument, named `syncToNetwork` is a boolean that, if `false`, indicates that the associated sync-adapter should not be run. Listing 7.15 demonstrates the trivial change in the code necessary to prevent sync-adapter run when the dataset change is caused by a network update.

Listing 7.15   **Notifying a Sync-Adapter of Dataset Change**

```
public Uri insert(@NonNull Uri uri, ContentValues vals) {
  long pk = getDb().insert(TABLE, NULLABLE_COL, vals);

  if (0 > pk) { return null; }

  uri = uri.buildUpon().appendPath(String.valueOf(pk)).build();
  getContext().getContentResolver().notifyChange(uri, null, !fromNet(url);

  return uri;
}
```

When the sync-adapter updates the database, it does so with a URI that appends a query parameter. The `fromNet` method checks for the presence of that query parameter and prevents a sync-adapter run when it is present.

Table 7.6 adds the sync-adapter to the scorecard. Where applicable, sync-adapters are very, very appealing, despite their overhead.

Table 7.6   **The Scorecard: Sync-Adapter**

Framework	Thread-safe	Lifecycle-aware	Process priority-aware	Power-thrifty
Timer and TimerTask	NA	NA	NA	NA
Looper/Handler	1	0	0	1
Service-based Scheduler	3	2	3	2
AlarmManger/ IntentService	4	4	4	3
Sync-adapter	5	5	4	4

The JobScheduler

The JobScheduler was introduced in Android API level 21, Lollipop. Its chief limitation is that because it is powered by a system service, there is no way to back-port its functionality to earlier versions of Android. At the time of this writing, the JobScheduler is available on more than a quarter of active Android devices. That number is sure to increase in the future.

The high-level concept that motivates the design of the JobScheduler is a much finer-grained control over the scheduling of asynchronous tasks. Tasks are no longer simply periodic. Instead, each task is associated with a collection of predicates, all of which must be true, before the task can be executed. The architecture of the JobScheduler is somewhere between that of the sync-adapter and AlarmManager systems: It is powered by a long-running system service but is simpler and more flexible than a sync-adapter.

Running a JobScheduler task requires only three steps:

- Make the task accessible to the JobScheduler.
- Schedule the task.
- Implement the task.

Making a task accessible to the JobScheduler is as simple as adding a canonical permission, `android.permission.BIND_JOB_SERVICE`, to a service component that is a subclass of the abstract class `JobService`. Listing 7.16 illustrates the declaration of the service in the manifest.

Listing 7.16   **A JobSchedule Service**

```
<service
  android:name=".scheduler.SimpleJobService"
  android:permission="android.permission.BIND_JOB_SERVICE" />
```

Note that unlike the sync-adapter, this declaration does not automatically cause any tasks to be scheduled. This declaration simply makes the Service accessible to the JobScheduler in case it is scheduled dynamically by the running application.

Scheduling a Task

Scheduling is what the JobScheduler is all about. As a system-level process, the JobScheduler has global information about device power, connectivity, and the behaviors of other applications. Its decisions about when a task should be run are considerably more astute than any other scheduler discussed so far. In addition to globally batching tasks, it offers developers several other methods for reducing the impact of a periodic task on both power and monetary budgets.

Much of the code required to schedule a JobScheduler task will look familiar. Listing 7.17 is an example.

Listing 7.17   **Scheduing a JobScheduler Task**

```
public class SimpleJobService extends JobService {

  // ...

  private static final String PARAM_TASK_TYPE = "SimpleJobService.TASK";
  private static final int SAMPLE_TASK = -1;

  private static final AtomicInteger JOB_ID = new AtomicInteger();

  public static void startSampleTask(Context ctxt) {
    JobScheduler js = (JobScheduler)
      ctxt.getSystemService(Context.JOB_SCHEDULER_SERVICE);

    cancelAllSampleTasks(js);

    PersistableBundle extras = new PersistableBundle();
    extras.putInt(PARAM_TASK_TYPE, SAMPLE_TASK);

    Resources rez = ctxt.getResources();
    int intervalSecs = 1000 * rez.getInteger(R.integer.sample_task_interval);

    js.schedule(
      new JobInfo.Builder(
        JOB_ID.getAndIncrement(),
        new ComponentName(ctxt, SimpleJobService.class))
        .setExtras(extras)
        .setBackoffCriteria(intervalSecs / 2, JobInfo.BACKOFF_POLICY_EXPONENTIAL)
        .setPeriodic(intervalSecs)
        .setPersisted(true)
        .setRequiresCharging(true)
        .setRequiredNetworkType(JobInfo.NETWORK_TYPE_UNMETERED)
        .build());
  }

  public static void cancelAllSampleTasks(Context ctxt) {
    cancelAllSampleTasks(
      (JobScheduler)ctxt.getSystemService(Context.JOB_SCHEDULER_SERVICE));
  }

  private static void cancelAllSampleTasks(JobScheduler js) {
    List<JobInfo> jobs = js.getAllPendingJobs();
```

```
    for (JobInfo job : jobs) {
      PersistableBundle extras = job.getExtras();
      if ((null != extras) && (extras.getInt(PARAM_TASK_TYPE, 0) == SAMPLE_TASK)) {
        js.cancel(job.getId());
      }
    }
  }

  // ...
}
```

As usual, a call to `getSystemService` retrieves a reference to system service—in this case, a JobService. As with the AlarmManager, this reference is actually a thin wrapper over a Binder IPC connection to a separate application that contains the system service. JobScheduler tasks are scheduled by calling its `schedule` method with an instance of the class `JobInfo`. The `JobInfo` instance in turn identifies the job to be run and the conditions under which to run it.

JobInfo objects are immutable, parcelable, and are constructed using the builder pattern. Their parameters are well documented and include everything necessary to schedule a periodic task. There are, in addition, several pleasant surprises.

First, note that the JobScheduler makes it dead simple to schedule tasks on criteria that are difficult or even impossible to use with the other periodic scheduling mechanisms. The task scheduled in Listing 7.17 will run only when the device is connected to both a power source and an unmetered (probably wifi) network. The JobScheduler's capability to schedule on these important conditions is its most attractive feature.

Next, note that the JobScheduler implements back-off. An application-wide, standard implementation of back-off and retry is one common reason for creating a homebrew execution service, as mentioned early in this chapter. The JobScheduler implements two back-off strategies, linear and exponential, right out of the box.

Although not demonstrated in Listing 7.17, the JobScheduler also supports deadlines. A deadline is a maximum amount of time after which the associated task will be run, regardless of whether or not other conditions have been met. Deadlines are only useful for one-shot tasks and cannot be used for periodic tasks.

Finally, notice that JobScheduler schedules can be persistent. A persistent task survives not only process boundaries but also power cycles. Because an application with a persistent JobScheduler task can restart itself automatically when the device is powered on, scheduling a persistent task is the equivalent of receiving the `BOOT_COMPLETED` broadcast intent. For this reason, only applications that hold the `RECEIVE_BOOT_COMPLETED` permission are enabled to schedule a persistent task.

As usual, any custom arguments to be passed from the scheduler to a running task must be marshaled into a Bundle and passed as "extras." In Listing 7.17, the extras mechanism is used as it was in the AlarmManager example earlier, to identify a specific task to be run.

The constructor for the JobInfo object takes the two arguments that define the task to be run. The first is an integer that is the unique identifier for the task. It serves exactly the same purpose as did the task ID supplied in the creation of the PendingIntent in Listing 7.3. When it becomes necessary to select a specific task—to cancel it, for instance—this integer identifies it uniquely. It is up to the code to assure that the ID actually is unique. Listing 7.18 uses an AtomicInteger.

The second argument to the constructor is something new. JobScheduler tasks are created dynamically and not statically set up in the manifest (as were sync-adapters). A JobInfo object contains a ComponentName. The component name completely specifies the Java class that implements the task to be run and the application that contains it.

As described at the beginning of this section, the task must be a Service component: it must be declared in the manifest, it must be a subclass of JobService, and it must be accessible, as shown in Listing 7.16. Any such accessible service, though, can be scheduled or have its schedule cancelled at any time. A JobInfo object is the only link between a set of scheduling conditions and the name of the service component that contains the task to be run.

Running a Task

Figure 7.2, similar to Figure 7.1, diagrams the process by which the JobScheduler runs a task.

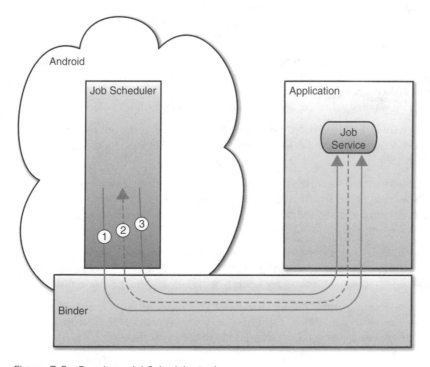

Figure 7.2   Running a JobScheduler task

The process begins when the JobScheduler determines that the conditions under which a particular task is to be run have been met. Like the SyncManager, the JobScheduler is a separate, system-level application. It initiates an IPC connection to the application containing the service component named in the JobInfo record (arrow #1 in Figure 7.2). As usual, this can have the side effect of starting the application.

Note that, like the Service for a sync-adapter, the Service for JobScheduler task does not have to be exported. This is a security measure. A service that is not exported is not publicly visible and cannot be used by other applications. The JobScheduler, however, is a privileged application and can connect to the service, even though other applications cannot.

As with any bound service, the service component to which the JobScheduler connects is simply the factory that returns an IPC connection to the required object (arrow #2 in Figure 7.2). With a terse blurring of roles, the JobScheduler expects the service component, an instance of a subclass of JobService, to return an IPC connection to an instance of a subclass of JobService. In other words, in response to the connection request from the JobScheduler, the service component returns a proxy to itself. The JobService class is both the factory for tasks and also the implementation of those tasks. The JobScheduler, using the proxy, calls the JobService method onStartJob, to run it (arrow #3 in Figure 7.2).

The oddest feature of the JobScheduler is that the JobService proxies the call to onStartJob *back onto the main thread*. When the onStartJob method executes, it does so on the main thread! If the periodically scheduled task is something that takes time and should not run on the main thread, as is so often the case, it is necessary to use a Looper/Handler to get it back off.

The JobScheduler holds a wake-lock during the remote call to onStartJob. Obviously, though, that isn't sufficient in the case in which onStartJob must use a Looper/Handler to execute most of the task, asynchronously. The completion of the onStartJob method is, under those circumstances, in no way related to the completion of the actual scheduled task.

To support this scenario, the onStartJob method returns a boolean. If the return value is true, then the JobScheduler considers the job to be running and holds the wake-lock for it until a subsequent call to jobFinished.

This method of holding the wake-lock is much safer than the technique used for the IntentService. The wake-lock is actually being held by a relatively secure system service. If the application that contains the scheduled task aborts for some reason, the system service, which is not affected, simply releases it.

The JobScheduler not only holds a wake-lock during the execution of a scheduled task, it also adjusts the process priority, giving it nearly the same precedence as the currently visible job. The process powering a scheduled task is very unlikely to be killed while the task is running.

The Android system, though, simply cannot guarantee that a running task will never be interrupted. Even a preferred application might have to be terminated, when other applications need resources. Lifecycles happen and the last word has to belong to the system. The

JobScheduler deals with this in a very curious way. When it needs to terminate a task, the JobScheduler calls the JobService method onStopJob. The documentation for this method says:

> You are solely responsible for the behaviour of your application upon receipt of this message; your app will likely start to misbehave if you ignore it.

So, how much time does an application have before it is considered to be "ignoring" the receipt of the message? What might constitute a "responsible" reaction, when the method is called? What kinds of "misbehavior" might be expected when the response is ignored?

The documentation provides no help for any of these questions. Instead, it points out one further problem. A task that is running on the main thread will itself block the reception of the onStopJob event (because it is enqueued on the main thread's MessageQueue)!

The existence of the onStopJob method recalls the deprecation of the stop method on the Thread class in Java. Java's designers realized that stop and its relatives suspend and resume were inherently unsafe and replaced them with the thread interruption protocol. That protocol, however, requires that the interrupted thread be cooperative and stop itself when interrupted. Android not only cannot depend on applications being cooperative, it must expect them to be uncooperative. These conflicting requirements have produced an ambiguous design.

Task Implementation

Listing 7.18 shows the implementation of a JobScheduler task.

Listing 7.18   **Implementing a JobScheduler Task**

```
public class SimpleJobService extends JobService {
  private final SparseArray<JobParameters> tasks = new SparseArray<>();

  @Inject
  volatile Lazy<SampleTask> sampleTask;

  private Handler taskHandler;
  private int currentTask;

  @Override
  @UiThread
  @SuppressWarnings("HandlerLeak")
  public void onCreate() {
    super.onCreate();

    HandlerThread thread = new HandlerThread("JobService");
    thread.start();

    DaggerTaskComponent.create().inject(this);
```

```java
    taskHandler = new Handler(thread.getLooper()) {
      @Override
      public void handleMessage(@NonNull Message msg) {
        switch (msg.what) {
          case SimpleJobService.MSG_START_TASK:
            startTask((JobParameters) msg.obj);
            break;
          default:
            Log.w(TAG, "unexpected message: " + msg.what);
        }
      }
    };
  }

  @Override
  @UiThread
  public void onDestroy() {
    taskHandler.getLooper().quitSafely();
    super.onDestroy();
  }

  @Override
  @UiThread
  public boolean onStartJob(JobParameters params) {
    enqueueTask(params);
    return true;
  }

  @Override
  @UiThread
  public boolean onStopJob(JobParameters params) {
    cancelTask(params);
    return true;
  }

  @WorkerThread
  void startTask(JobParameters params) {
    int op = dequeueTask(params);
    try {
      switch (op) {
        case SimpleJobService.SAMPLE_TASK:
          if (!Thread.currentThread().isInterrupted()) { sampleTask.get().run(); }
          break;
        default:
          Log.w(TAG, "unexpected op: " + op);
      }
    }
```

```
    finally {
      jobFinished(params, false);
    }
  }

  @UiThread
  private void enqueueTask(JobParameters params) {
    synchronized (tasks) {
      tasks.put(params.getJobId(), params);
      taskHandler.obtainMessage(MSG_START_TASK, params).sendToTarget();
    }
  }

  @UiThread
  private void cancelTask(JobParameters params) {
    int jobId = params.getJobId();
    synchronized (tasks) {
      if (currentTask == jobId) { taskHandler.getLooper().getThread().interrupt(); }
      else {
        JobParameters oParams = tasks.get(jobId);
        if (null == oParams) { return; }
        tasks.delete(jobId);
        taskHandler.removeMessages(MSG_START_TASK, oParams);
      }
    }
  }

  @WorkerThread
  private int dequeueTask(JobParameters params) {
    int jobId = params.getJobId();

    PersistableBundle extras = params.getExtras();
    if (null == extras) {
      Log.w(TAG, "null extras");
      return 0;
    }

    synchronized (tasks) {
      if (null == tasks.get(jobId)) { return 0; }
      tasks.delete(jobId);
      currentTask = jobId;
      Thread.interrupted(); // clear thread interrupts
    }

    return extras.getInt(SimpleJobService.PARAM_TASK_TYPE, 0);
  }
}
```

This is a disappointingly large piece of code. Much of it necessary simply to get scheduled tasks to run on a background thread. It is all a lot like the code from the Chapter 5, "Looper/Handler."

The implementation spawns only a single background thread. It cannot support multiple simultaneously scheduled tasks. This is a limitation that might well be unacceptable in some situations. A more fully featured implementation might have to farm tasks out instead, perhaps to a custom, Service-based scheduler.

Before considering such a thing, however, a developer would do well to consider what, exactly, it means to enqueue for later execution, a task that the JobScheduler thinks should execute right now. There is no way to guarantee the timely execution of any task. Clearly, if the hardware is already busy, no amount of clever code will help. If it is necessary to combine multiple schedulers, understanding the details of how they interact when they are linked in series, is essential to creating a rational design.

A call to onStartJob enqueues a message containing the task parameters on a Handler queue, for execution on a background thread. It also stores those parameters in a sparse array, by job id, for later reference.

When the message is processed on the background thread, it is dequeued, the opcode identified, and the corresponding task executed. This implementation, like the AlarmManager/IntentService code, uses a single service component to schedule multiple different types of tasks. This is not necessary, of course. Each task can be implemented as its own, separate service. A developer that chooses this path, though, will surely want to create a subclass of JobService that contains the substantial boilerplate evident in Listing 7.18.

Incidentally, there is also no reason that the JobScheduler can't use the AccountManager. Although there is no built-in support for it, a JobScheduler task could take advantage of the full flexibility of the AccountManager service, obtaining, authenticating, and using user accounts as necessary. There was, actually, a rumor, during the early days of Lollipop, that the SyncAdapter would be re-implemented on top of the JobScheduler to open access to its fine-grained scheduler.

Almost all the code in Listing 7.18, not devoted to moving requests to a background thread owes its existence to the requirement that tasks be stoppable. Even in this single threaded case, and not considering the complexities of stopping the actual running task, this is wildly complex.

When a call to onStopJob occurs—and this is a general observation—a task will be in one of two possible states. It will be waiting to execute, or it will be execution. The task must be stopped whichever of the two states it is in.

The cancelTask method looks for the task in the tasks array by id. If the task is waiting to execute, the JobParameter object with which it was originally enqueued is there and can be used in the Handler method removeMessage to delete the queued task.

If, however, the task is currently running, its task id is stored in the data member `currentTask`. In this case, `cancelTask` sends an interrupt to the thread running the task. Tasks are expected to honor this interrupt and terminate.

Scoring the JobScheduler

The JobScheduler has some solid points in its favor. It has by far the best scheduling protocol of any of the schedulers examined here. The interface is fairly simple and the builder used to create task schedules makes it very easy to use. Tasks are scheduled with a global perspective and are thus intelligently clustered to save both power and money. This ability to conserve is enough to overcome most objections.

In addition, as the examples demonstrate, many of the things that manifest as uncomfortable warts in the other schedulers are simply built in here. The system manages wake-locks safely and gives the running task's process enough priority so that it has room to work.

The JobScheduler flexibility can be made even broader by creating multiple different schedules for a single task. With only some obvious extensions to the code in Listing 7.18, one could schedule a task to be run every ten minutes when connected to WiFi, every hour when connected by cell, and to notify the user if there is no connection for an entire day.

On the down side are the JobScheduler's curious predilection for running tasks on the main thread, and its crude and clumsy job cancellation protocol. Together they lead to a lot of complex, error prone, yet boring code.

Table 7.7 puts the JobScheduler into the table. The JobSchedule does some things very well.

Table 7.7 **The Scorecard: JobScheduler**

Framework	Thread-safe	Lifecycle-aware	Process priority-aware	Power-thrifty
Timer and TimerTask	NA	NA	NA	NA
Looper/Handler	1	0	0	1
Service-based Scheduler	3	2	3	2
AlarmManger/ IntentService	4	4	4	3
Sync-adapter	5	5	4	4
JobScheduler	3	5	5	5

Summary

This chapter examines a common concurrent paradigm, a periodically scheduled task, and several possible implementations in the Android environment. The final scorecard, Table 7.7, shows each framework along with ratings on the main requirements.

Perhaps the most important take-away not completely illustrated in the scorecard is that there is no single silver bullet. There are situations—frequent, ephemeral tasks—in which a Looper/Handler is the correct solution, and attempting to replace it with a sync-adapter would be laughable. Sometimes the right decision is to implement that custom Service-based scheduler because it's the only way to get the necessary control and flexibility. Even the most recent addition, the JobScheduler, is a trade-off.

There are other lessons, though. One is that sync-adapters are undervalued. Despite their substantial overhead and initial cost, sync-adapters are a brilliant solution to a very common application problem.

Another is that understanding wake-locks, process priority, and even the details of the hardware are important in creating a robust, delightful application.

8

Concurrency Tools

We shape our tools and then our tools shape us

Marshall McLuhan

The most important thing to notice about this chapter is that it is very, very short.

The Java language changed the world for developer tool-chains. Its strong static typing made possible the creation of powerful IDEs like Eclipse and IDEA. The power of these IDEs stems from the fact that they can analyze the source code, intermediate representations, and the byte-code binaries. Modern IDEs understand the deep structure of Java code and can perform complex operations like refactoring, jump to definition, and so on.

Without strong typing, it is much more difficult to implement such operations reliably. Even today, though most Java developers prefer structured IDEs, it is not uncommon to find dynamic language developers working with emacs, Sublime Text, or Vim. Without static typing, an IDE simply cannot offer that much more functionality than a simpler, lighter-weight editor.

Unfortunately, with respect to concurrency, Java is more like those dynamically typed languages. Even in constrained circumstances, it can be difficult to determine what threads might execute any give piece of code. It is in general impossible.

In this environment, the selection of tools available for verifying the correctness of concurrent code is small. The selection of tools available for analyzing and debugging an application with a concurrency error is even worse.

Static Analysis

Static analysis tools inspect code either before or after compilation, and attempt to discover problems and inconsistencies. In general, these tools prove statements about the code by applying collections of rules. Because Java's wealth of strong static typing information is available to these rules, they can be pretty effective. Also, because they analyze the structure of the code, they do not require that a one-in-a-million bug actually must occur to find it.

They cannot, of course, find all problems. But they can find many problems! Releasing an application or a library without running it through one or more static analysis tools makes no more sense than sending out your resume without running it through a spell-checker.

Several static analysis tools are available. Many of them are chiefly directed at revealing security issues. Many require the purchase of some kind of license—something that many development houses find to be an entirely reasonable investment. Among the common for-profit static analysis tools that have at least some concurrency analysis capabilities are HP Fortify, SonarQube, and ThreadSafe.

Android Studio

Android Studio has its own built-in static analysis tools (see Figure 8.1). Called Inspections, they are configured from a pane in the standard Preferences dialog (under Editor > Inspections).

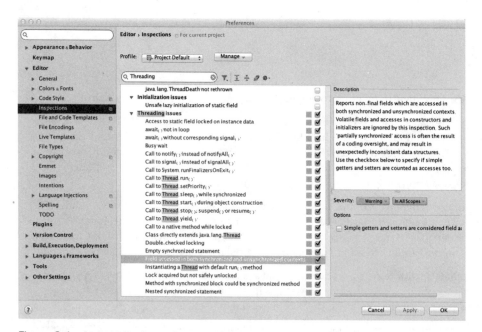

Figure 8.1   Android Studio concurrency inspections

Inspections are very well integrated into Android Studio. Inspection violations show up as warnings in the right gutter of the editor, as shown in Figure 8.2. A developer could do worse than turning all the concurrency-related inspections on and, at the very least, understanding the exact cause of each warning they generate.

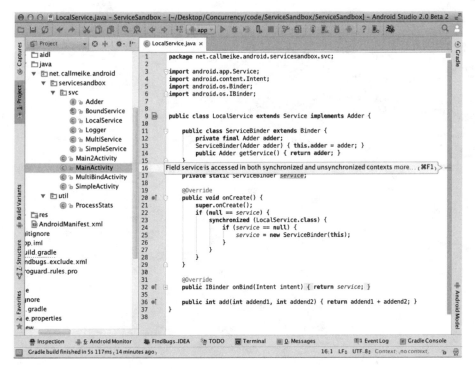

Figure 8.2   An Android Studio inspection

Findbugs

Findbugs, from the University of Maryland, is useful and free. It is available as a plugin for most common IDEs and build systems, including Gradle, IDEA (Android Studio), and Eclipse.

In addition to other checks, Findbugs inspects code for more than 40 concurrency-related issues. Some of the issues are simple "gottchas," such as calling the `run` method of a thread or synchronizing on a boxed primitive. Findbugs can also catch trickier errors, even some that humans are likely to miss.

Findbugs with Android Studio

Configuring Findbugs for Android Studio is only slightly more difficult than installing the plugin. Using Studio's standard plugin installation dialog, browse repositories for the plugin, as illustrated in Figure 8.3.

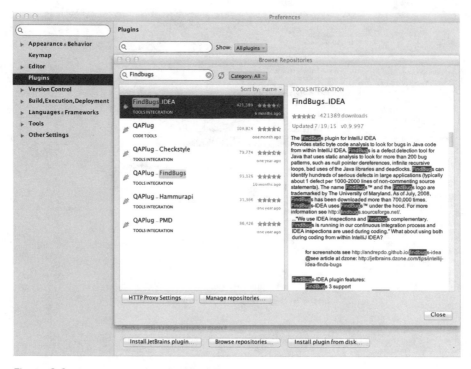

Figure 8.3   Installing the Android Studio Findbugs plugin

Once the plugin is installed, it must be configured. There should now be an entry for it under Other Settings in the Preferences dialog, as shown in Figure 8.4.

In this case, Findbugs has been configured to show only Multithreaded Correctness issues. It can make sense to run other checks as well.

Note that the level for "Minimum confidence to report" has been set to **Low**. Although it is important to keep the noise of false-positives down, it is a good idea, especially when restricting the search to concurrency issues, to start by reporting all potential issues and filtering only if it is necessary to do so.

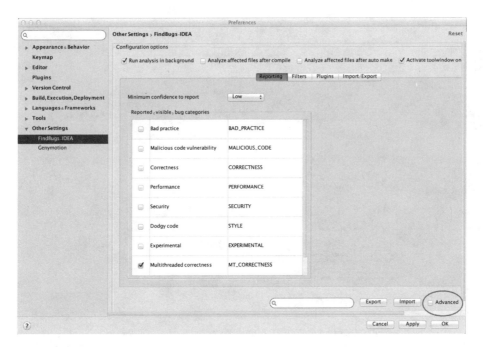

Figure 8.4   Configuring the Findbugs plugin

Even more important is the Advanced button on the lower right. Checking it enables access to the otherwise invisible configuration page, shown in Figure 8.5.

This page gives access to a couple of important things. A slider on the top left enables raising the analysis effort to Maximal. Because that means that it takes significant time for Findbugs to run, it is probably also a good idea to check the box that causes Findbugs to run in background.

Finally, this page enables turning detectors off and on individually. This is useful when considering the JCIP annotations, which are described in the next section.

As the last step in configuring the plugin, be sure to include all the available detectors. From the **Plugin** tab, check all the plugins as shown in Figure 8.6. The Android detectors are of particular interest. Any detectors that prove uninteresting can be excluded later.

Click **OK** to complete the configuration process.

Findbugs is now ready to run.

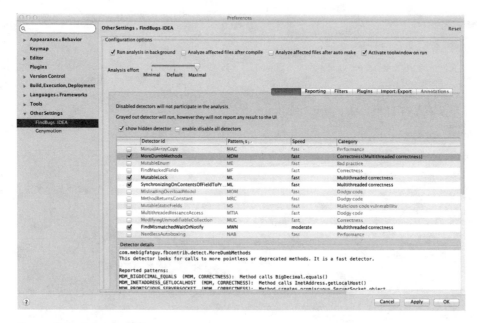

Figure 8.5   Advanced Findbugs plugin configuration

Figure 8.6   Installing detectors

Listing 8.1 shows some example code for analysis. Obviously, it contains several errors. To analyze a project with Findbugs, first select **Findbugs** and click **Analyze Project Files** from IDEA's **Analyze** menu. Figure 8.7 shows the results.

Listing 8.1 **Successful Findbugs Example**

```java
public class LocalService extends Service implements Adder {

  public class ServiceBinder extends Binder {
    private final Adder adder;
    ServiceBinder(Adder adder) { this.adder = adder; }
    public Adder getService() { return adder; }
  }

  private ServiceBinder service;

  @Override
  public void onCreate() {
    super.onCreate();
    if (service == null) {
      synchronized (this) {
        if (service == null) {
          service = new ServiceBinder(this);
        }
      }
    }
  }

  @Override
  public IBinder onBind(Intent intent) {
    return service;
  }

  public int add(int addend1, int addend2) { return addend1 + addend2; }
}
```

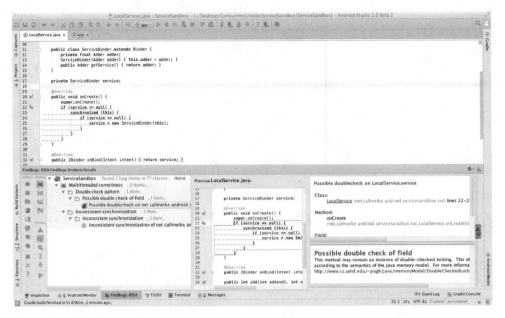

Figure 8.7   The FindBugs pane

In this particular case, Findbugs correctly identifies both double-check locking and inconsistently synchronized access to the variable `service` as errors.

Although a powerful tool, Findbugs is not all-seeing. It misses the fact that there is no need for any synchronization at all in the code in Listing 8.1. Because all the methods there are guaranteed to run on a single thread—the main thread—the synchronized block is simply unnecessary.

Listing 8.2 is nearly identical to Listing 8.1. In fact, it contains exactly the same errors. Because the variable `service` is now static and the order of comparison is reversed in the first check of the double-check lock, Findbugs erroneously give this code a completely clean bill of health.

Listing 8.2   **Findbugs Fail**

```
public class LocalService extends Service implements Adder {

  public class ServiceBinder extends Binder {
    private final Adder adder;
    ServiceBinder(Adder adder) { this.adder = adder; }
    public Adder getService() { return adder; }
  }
```

```
private static ServiceBinder service; // static variable

@Override
public void onCreate() {
  super.onCreate();
  if (null == service) { // reversed comparison
    synchronized (LocalService.class) {
      if (service == null) {
        service = new ServiceBinder(this);
      }
    }
  }
}

@Override
public IBinder onBind(Intent intent) {
  return service;
}

public int add(int addend1, int addend2) { return addend1 + addend2; }
}
```

> **Note**
>
> You **must** build your project to analyze it with Findbugs!
>
> Findbugs analyzes the compiled Java bytecode. For it to analyze changes in the source code, that code must be recompiled. In IDEA, select **Rebuild Project** from the **Build** menu.

Findbugs with Gradle

An important use for static analysis is as part of a continuous integration system. Even in codebases in which it takes double-digit minutes to run a full Findbugs analysis, running it as part of the pre-commit regimen is an excellent backstop against careless oversight.

To do this, Findbugs must be incorporated into the build system. For Android, that means Gradle.

As of version 2.10, Gradle provides basic Findbugs support. Integrating that support with an Android project requires a little Gradle hacking. Listing 8.3's template can be included and added to the `build.gradle` file for almost any Android project. It adds Findbugs tasks for all the project's build variants.

Listing 8.3   **Findbugs in Gradle**

```
apply plugin: 'findbugs'

findbugs { toolVersion = "3.0.1" }

afterEvaluate {
  def variants = plugins.hasPlugin('com.android.application')
    ? android.applicationVariants
    : android.libraryVariants

  variants.each { variant ->
    def task = tasks.create("findbugs${variant.name.capitalize()}", FindBugs)

    task.group = 'verification'
    task.description = "Run FindBugs on ${variant.description}."

    def variantCompile = variant.javaCompile

    task.dependsOn(variantCompile)
    tasks.getByName('check').dependsOn(task)
        .
    task.classes = fileTree(variantCompile.destinationDir)
    task.source = variantCompile.source
    task.classpath
      = variantCompile.classpath.plus(project.files(android.bootClasspath))

    task.effort = 'max'
    task.reportLevel = 'low'
    task.ignoreFailures = false

    task.excludeFilter = file("findbugs-exclude.xml")
    task.reports {
      xml { enabled = false }
      html { enabled = true }
    }
  }
}
```

The code in Listing 8.3 generates a new Gradle task for each build variant. Each new task runs Findbugs for that variant. The listing explicitly uses the version of Findbugs current at the time of this writing, version 3.0.1.

As shown, this code causes those new tasks to fail with a Findbugs error. This is probably desirable in the context of a build job. To ignore failures, simply change the sense of the `ignoreFailures` boolean.

The code in Listing 8.3 also depends on a Findbugs configuration file called findbugs-exclude.xml. Android projects contain a lot of auto-generated code that plays fast and loose with coding standards, making such an exclusion file nearly essential. Listing 8.4 gives a minimal example of such a file. There I give more information on creating an excludes file, and on configuring other Findbugs parameters in the official on-line documentation, here: http://findbugs.sourceforge.net/manual/index.html.

Listing 8.4   **A Minimum Findbugs Filter**

```
<FindBugsFilter>
  <Match>
    <Class name="~.*R\$.*"/>
  </Match>
  <Match>
    <Class name="~.*Manifest\$.*"/>
  </Match>
</FindBugsFilter>
```

Annotations

Annotations are an extension of basic static analysis. They are an additional tool that gives hints to a static analyzer, enabling it to make better analyses.

In the development environment, Android application code is compiled against a library of stubs. Because the stubs are empty and do not contain the actual implementations of the library methods, static analyzers cannot see that actual code and are severely constrained.

As an example, there is no way that a static analysis tool can figure out that the `onHandleIntent` method of an `IntentService` is run on a different thread from its `onCreate` method. This presents the opportunity for an extremely common error, initializing a field in `onCreate` and then accessing it from `onHandleIntent` without proper synchronization. Hints provided by annotations come very close to eliminating this problem.

JCIR Annotations

As noted earlier, anyone writing any concurrent code in Java should have a copy of the most excellent *Java Concurrency in Practice* (Göetz, 2006) near her desk. Among the many good things to come from that book is a proposal for a set of concurrency-related annotations.

These annotations, commonly referred to as the JCIP annotations, were included in Java Specification Request (JSR) 305:

- `@GuardedBy` (`"guard-variable"`): All access to the following declaration should be synchronized on *guard-variable*.

- `@Immutable`: Instances of the annotated type are immutable.

- `@NotThreadSafe`: An object that is not thread-safe. Objects are assumed to be not thread-safe, so this annotation is mostly documentation.

- `@ThreadSafe`: Instance of this type can be used safely by multiple threads, concurrently.

Although JSR-305 seems to have stalled, several static analysis tools including Findbugs support, or partially support, these annotations. At the time of this writing, they seem to be supported in Android Studio both by the FindBugs Plugin and by native Inspections. The Android Studio Findbugs plugin is much less reliable.

Support Library Annotations

Of more interest to Android developers are the Android-specific annotations defined in Google's Android support library. There are several of them, supported by both Eclipse and Android Studio. The annotations that relate to concurrency are:

- `@UIThread`: The annotated method is intended to run only on the main thread.

- `@MainThread`: This is normally identical to `@UIThread`. According to the documentation, although there is never more than one main thread, some applications run entire alternate UIs on threads other than this main thread. The documentation advises using `@MainThread` to annotate lifecycle methods (for example, `onCreate` and `onResume`) and `@UIThread` to annotate specifically UI-related methods (`onMeasure` and `onDraw`).

- `@BinderThread`: The annotated method runs on a Binder thread, as mentioned in Chapter 6, "Services, Processes, and IPC."

- `@WorkerThread`: The annotated method runs on a thread not mentioned above. The `doInBackground` method from `AsyncTask`, and the `onHandleIntent` method from `IntentService` are examples of methods annotated with `@WorkerThread`.

All the code examples in this book use these annotations whenever relevant.

These annotations make somewhat weaker assertions about the code they annotate than the JCIP annotations do. The thing that makes these annotations powerful is that the stubbed version of the Android framework, against which developers build their applications, has been annotated with them. The code in Listing 8.5 demonstrates this.

Listing 8.5 **Using the Android Support Annotations**

```
public class SimpleIntentService extends IntentService {

  // ...

  @Override
  protected void onHandleIntent(Intent intent) {
    doSomething();  // !!! error
  }

  @MainThread
  private void doSomething() {}
}
```

The call to doSomething is flagged as an error. Even though the onHandleIntent method in this listing is not annotated, the overridden method is annotated with the @WorkerThread annotation in the base class, IntentService. The call to the @MainThread annotated method from a @WorkerThread annotated method is obviously an error.

The Gradle lint task checks Android Support Annotations and can be used to run these checks for continuous integration.

Assertions

Static analysis only goes so far. Some concurrency testing must be done at runtime.

An obvious tool for making runtime concurrency checks is Java's assert statement. It was possible to enable Java assertions in older versions of Android by entering the command:

```
setprop debug.assert 1
```

from the ADB (Android Debug Bridge) command line. The setting can be made persistent by including it in the file:

```
/data/local.prop
```

Unfortunately, though, as of API level 22 or so, Java assertions no longer work at all. They are completely unsupported as of this writing in the new Android runtime, ART.

Although that eliminates an obvious tool, it doesn't eliminate the possibility of creating runtime concurrency checks. The static methods in the JUnit Assert class are one convenient way of enforcing class invariants. When using them, be careful not to drag the entire JUnit suite into the application. Use only junit.framework.Assert and, if necessary, use minification (ProGuard) to eliminate unneeded classes.

If all else fails, a simple `if` statement will suffice:

```
if (!Looper.getMainLooper().getThread().equals(Thread.currentThread()) {
    throw new AssertionError(
        "attempt to run this thing from other than the main thread");
}
```

The important decision with respect to assertions is what to do with them when they occur. This decision is often religious, and the choice made by any particular developer or team probably will not be affected by any discussion here. Most development teams, however, do agree on three goals for assertions:

- Report the error to someone that can fix it.

- Don't do any permanent damage.

- Don't advertise the problem.

Perhaps the most common alternative is simply to enable assertions only during testing and to turn them off in production. Cross your fingers and hope for the best.

At the other end of the spectrum, an application with a good failure reporting and restart mechanism, such as Crashlytics, Flurry, and so on, might simply abort on an exception. In some ways this is ideal: the problem is reported and the application does not continue running in an unknown state. It usually has the downside, however, of being quite visible to the user.

Somewhere in between lies the gray area of reporting the error with some kind of event reporter, and attempting recovery.

Conclusion and Best Practices

Nearly every Android developer will have to deal with concurrent code. Doing so is difficult, finicky, and incredibly easy to get wrong. The tools available to support the work are no more than adequate.

There are some best practices that can make code more robust and less susceptible to strange, difficult-to-diagnose errors.

- Immutable objects are simple and thread-safe. Although some developers find the clutter annoying, nailing every possible value down with a final modifier can make code much easier to manage. Using the Builder pattern is a great way to create immutable objects.

- Code that runs on a single thread, whatever thread that happens to be, is easy to understand. If multithreading is necessary, try to keep it contained. Bury it in the framework so that most developers need not even be aware of it.

- As a corollary to the preceding point, try to make Java classes and source files single-threaded. Source files that are too big to fit into a single editor screen, and that contain methods that run on different threads, are accidents waiting to happen.

- If it is necessary to have methods from a single class executed on multiple threads, annotate or comment those methods. There is *nothing* in the code itself that gives any indication of the threading strategy. The frequently heard excuse that "the code is the comment" is utterly inapplicable for multithreaded code.

- Review multithreaded code very carefully. A fresh pair of eyes can often spot a tiny oversight in even the best-planned and well-executed designs.

- Use static analysis. Set the report criteria on the tool as low as possible and take the time to understand every anomaly it reports. Use multiple tools if possible. Annotate!

- Get as much code as you can out of Activities (and Fragments). An Activity is the manager for a page. It shouldn't contain business logic.

- Get as much code as you can out of Android components in general. Use one of the modern UI patterns (Model-View-ViewModel, Model-View-Presenter) to get display logic out of your Activity. Keep your Services as the factories they should be and inject the implementation, either by hand or using an IoC (Inversion of Control) framework. Testing will be much easier.

Create a few simple, clear execution strategies for long-running tasks, and then use them consistently. Where possible, use runtime assertions to validate them. Make it easy and routine to follow architecture.

Good luck!

Bibliography

Göetz, Brian, et al., *Java Concurrency in Practice*. Upper Saddle River, NJ: Addison-Wesley Professional, 2006.

Griffiths, Dawn, and David Griffiths, *Head First Android Development*, 1st Edition. Sebastapol, CA: O'Reilly Media, 2015.

Mednieks, Zigurd, Laird Dornin, Blake Meike, and Masumi Nakamura, *Programming Android*, 2nd Edition. Sebastapol, CA: O'Reilly Media, 2012.

Moore, Gordon E., "Cramming More Components onto Integrated Circuits," *Electronics*, April 19, 1965, 114–117.

Murphy, Mark, "The Busy Coder's Guide to Android Development," CommonsWare, LLC, 2009.

von Neumann, John. "First Draft of a Report on the EDVAC," Contract No. W-670-ORD-4926 Between the United States Army Ordnance Department and the University of Pennsylvania, Moore School of Electrical Engineering, University of Pennsylvania, June 30, 1945.

Index